Palo Alto Cortex XSOAR

A Practical Guide

First Edition, 2021

Jithin Aby Alex

About the Author

Jithin Aby Alex, CISSP, CEH, PCSAE
Security Professional, having experience in managing security operations, implementing and handling major security solutions and products in various environments and regions. I have used my experience, professional connections and publicly available information for writing this book. Personally, I thank you for purchasing this book and thanks for the support. I hope this book will be informative to you and I wish you all the best.
Please visit www.jaacostan.com for my articles and technical write-ups.

Copyright © Jithin Aby Alex

First Edition, 2021

"Happiness is having a coworker who becomes a friend"
Dedicated to my Friends

Contents

How to Use this book?

This book is a beginner friendly, step by step practical guide that helps you to understand and learn Palo Alto Cortex XSOAR from scratch. No previous knowledge about the product is required and I have explained all the important topics step by step, with screenshots. It will be easy to follow if you have a basic understanding about Incident Response and SOC environment. However, I have tried to explain everything in a very simple and easy manner.

It is recommended to follow this book from top to down, in order. Don't skip any chapters or else you might find it difficult to understand the concepts.

Install the community edition of Cortex XSOAR and practice the tasks along with the reading. Hands-on is very much important and without the practice, you cannot master Cortex XSOAR.

This page intentionally left blank.

1.Introduction

Before getting deep dive in to the Palo Alto Cortex XSOAR, let's go through some basic security concepts. As Security professionals, we all do have an idea about SOC operations and Incident Management. However, let have a quick refresher to set the foundations.

1.1 What is Security Incident Management?

Incident handling is the action plan for dealing with computer security incidents or events such as hacking, intrusions, data theft, policy violations. All organizations must have and follow a proper Incident Handling policy which must be authorized by the top management of the organization. Security incident includes a broad spectrum of events which will affect the organization and its clients, customers in the form of availability, data loss, monetary loss, reputation loss or intellectual property loss etc. Complete prevention of incidents is nearly impossible however with having a proper Security Incident Handling policy, the organization can minimize the impact of an incident and prevent repetitive incidents.

A Security Incident Handling process consists of well documented policies and procedures, qualified teams and personnel, relevant tools, awareness and most importantly the support from the top-level management of the organization. All policies must comply with the applicable laws of the region or the country. The Incident handling framework consists of Preparation, Identification of an Incident, Containment, Incident Eradication, Recovery and Lessons Learned/Follow-up.

1.2 What is a Security Operations Centre (SOC)?

As security professionals, our job is to reduce the level of risk to our organization from cyber security threats. To do this we use various tools and solutions to detect and prevent the attack attempts by various malicious actors. And normally we perform these operations from a centralized facility known as a Security Operations Centre (SOC). The SOC consists of a team of skilled security professionals that are dedicated to monitoring and analyzing activity on networks, servers, endpoints, databases, applications, websites, and other systems that connect to your network infrastructure. The SOC objective is to detect, analyze, and respond to cybersecurity incidents using a combination of technology solutions and a set of processes to help mitigate the incidents. And for this, there should be a proper documented Incident Response plan in place.

The major functions of SOC are,

1) Incident Identification: Identify the suspicious events and create an Incident ticket.
2) Incident Investigation: Investigate the incident for the impact and identify the root cause.
3) Incident Mitigation: Stop the attack by fixing the vulnerabilities that were exploited.

4) Continuous Improvement: Improve the operations to keep up with changing and emerging threats.

A security sounded organization ideally implement a multi-layer security mechanism, also known as Defense in Depth (DiD). DiD must cover all aspects of security from infrastructure security to the end user security. The common tools which we can find in such environment are firewalls, Intrusion Prevention Systems, Web Application Firewalls, Network Access control solutions, Identity and Access Management solutions, Endpoint security etc. The more tools, the more complicated architecture it will be. These all tools generate a lot of information and to process and correlate, enterprises usually use SIEM tools such as Splunk, QRadar etc. The analysts, those are working from the SOC constantly monitors the alerts and trigger the Incident Response plan in the case of a suspicious event. So, how many such alerts are generated per minute? Depends up on the size of the organization, it varies from ten to thousands. Monitoring and responding to these alerts are a tedious task and many of such alerts could be false positive. However, once the Incident Response is triggered, it consumes time and resource to perform the investigation. Hence it is very important to reduce the number of false alerts to keep things efficient.

Another important aspect is the knowledge and skillset of the Security Analysts. Not all are equal and the ability of people to respond and handle a particular incident might varies as well. Also, there are high chances of overlooking the alerts. Human error plays an important role in almost every data breached and Cybersecurity attacks.

The major problems that a SOC faces are mentioned below,
1) Alert Fatigue due to a large number of false positives.
2) Analysts lack skill and knowledge, which eventually led to human errors.
3) Large number of tools which might delay the detection and investigation process.
4) Gaps in collaboration. Incident investigation involves different teams and therefore a coordinated work is vital for a proper incident investigation and its closure.

1.3 What is SOAR?

SOAR stands for Security Orchestration, Automation and Response. Gartner defines a SOAR solution as, *technologies that enable organizations to collect inputs monitored by the security operations team. For example, alerts from the SIEM system and other security technologies — where incident analysis and triage can be performed by leveraging a combination of human and machine power — help define, prioritize and drive standardized incident response activities. SOAR tools allow an organization to define incident analysis and response procedures in a digital workflow format*

SOAR solution ingests events/alerts from external sources such as SIEMs, log servers, monitoring tools, other security tools like Firewalls, IPS etc.) and respond to these alerts by executing an automated process-driven playbook and thereby performing the Incident Investigation in an automated, quick and organized manner. The playbooks coordinate across technologies, security teams, and external users to gather information and to take action in a decisive way. In other terms, SOAR is a centralized security orchestration and Automation solution to accelerate incident response and increase analyst productivity.

A SOAR platform integrates your organization's security and monitoring tools, helping you centralize, standardize your incident handing processes. It automatically correlates security alerts from external sources against threat intelligence feeds for bad indicators, integrates malware analysis into incidents after detonating in a sandbox or submitting to a third party for analysis.

1.4 Palo Alto Cortex XSOAR

The SOAR product offering from Palo Alto networks is known as Cortex XSOAR.

As per Palo Alto documentation, *Cortex™ XSOAR is a comprehensive security orchestration, automation and response (SOAR) platform that unifies case management, automation, real-time collaboration and threat intel management to serve security teams across the incident lifecycle.*

Cortex XSOAR focuses on the following areas,
1) Security Orchestration and Automation
2) Case Management
3) Collaboration and Learning
4) Threat Intel Management

Note: The product was formerly known as Demisto SOAR. In 2019, Palo Alto Networks acquired Demisto and later named the product to Cortex XSOAR.

The features and benefits of Cortex XSOAR includes,
- **Integrations and Extensible Platform:** Built-in security product integrations and SDK's. Supports a large number of third-party integrations which can be easily installed from the trusted Marketplace directly from the XSOAR GUI.
- **Visual Playbook Editor:** Easy-to-build playbooks with thousands of pre-built functions and offers a sandboxed environment knows as Playground to test the playbook functionalities.
- **Quick response:** Automated workflows and remediation using playbooks.
- **Virtual War Room:** Conduct joint investigations and run security commands in a real-time collaborated environment, quicker incident resolution times and better SOC efficiency.
- **Case Management:** Create and assign cases to Analysts.

- **Evidence Board:** An evidence timeline to reconstruct attack chains
- **Dashboards and Reports:** Fully customizable dashboards and reports.

- **Indicator Repository:** All indicators are auto-discovered and correlated across incidents. Supports threat intel management and configure feeds to enrich the indicators.

- **Machine Learning:** DBot is a ML bot, trains on data to generate insights.

- Supports various deployment options from standalone to cloud, hosted.

- Supports Multi-Tenants and thereby enables MSSP's to provide improved SOC as a Service to the customers.

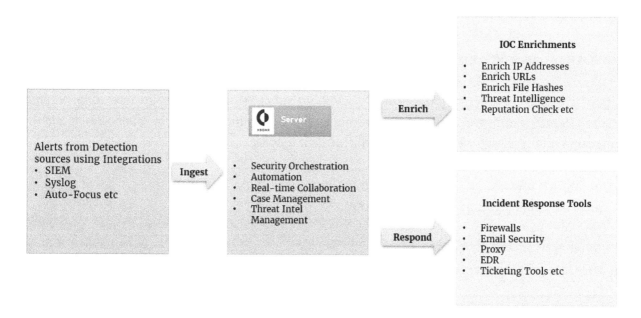

Image: Cortex XSOAR ecosystem

Let's see briefly how Cortex XSOAR works. Assume a user received a Phishing mail in an organization. The link in the phishing mail was pointing to a malicious URL. The mail was detected by the endpoint security installed in the user machine, as well as it was detected by the email security gateway. The detection logs are sent to the SIEM. SIEM is further integrated with Cortex XSOAR. XSOAR ingests the alert from the SIEM and automatically create a Phishing Incident. Each incident type has an associated playbook that consists of a series of tasks that has to be perform with respect to the incident investigation.

For example, the mail has to be inspected, the malicious URL mentioned inside the phishing email should be blocked at the firewall level. Also, the analyst might need to gather some data from the end user also. So, based on the organization's Phishing Incident response SOP, it involves a large number of tasks that has to be performed in an organized manner based on its priority. If this is performed manually, it could take hour(s) to complete the investigation and close the incident.

So now with Cortex XSOAR, the incident can be assigned to the best matching analyst automatically based on the case history and work load, and the associated playbook for Phishing incident gets triggered as well, as the part of investigation. Data gathering and information enrichment can be done automatically by the defined playbook. Analyst can do any manual task from the War-room if needed and can attach evidences. Also, can communicate with other analysts for any additional inputs. If defined in the playbook, the playbook can also perform the task to communicate with the organization's firewall and automatically push a rule to block the malicious URL. Once all playbook tasks are completed, the incident can be closed and generate the incident report either manually or automated.

This is just an example, but Cortex XSOAR can perform much more and complex tasks that this. By integrating different security solutions and tools, you can automate almost every security operational task with the help of Cortex XSOAR.

I will be explaining the important features of Cortex XSOAR with sample use-cases in the following chapters. Starting with the architecture and deployment options, then how to install and configure Cortex XSOAR, create integrations, incident types, layouts and Incidents. The core of every incident investigation is the Playbook. I will be explaining how to plan, develop and use a playbook for an incident investigation. Let's jump in.

This page intentionally left blank.

2. Cortex XSOAR Hardware and Software requirements

2.1 Deployment Options.

You can deploy Palo Alto Cortex XSOAR in four ways.

1) On-Premises
You can install Cortex XSOAR on a VM or bare-metal servers. In this installation model, the customer provisions, installs, configures, and maintains all aspects of the system while Palo Alto Networks provides support based on licensing. The supported operating systems to install Cortex XSOAR and the minimum hardware requirements are mentioned in the next section.

2) Hosted Cloud
In this model, Palo Alto Networks provisions and maintains the customer's instance of the Cortex XSOAR server, which includes maintaining the OS, performing upgrades, providing high availability. The customer only needs to configure and maintain the Cortex SOAR from an application-layer level. Palo Alto Networks provides application support based on the license purchased. Only the Palo Alto Networks DevOps team has access to the OS. The cloud-hosted option is not a full security-as-a-service offering. After the cloud instance is deployed, the customer is responsible for all configuration, integration, and automation work required using the product's web console. At the time of writing this book, Palo Alto Networks provides Cortex XSOAR hosted-cloud instances on AWS only.

3) Private Cloud
Another installation model is Private Cloud, in which you can deploy Cortex XSOAR within your private cloud. Palo Alto Networks treats a private cloud deployment the same as an on-premises deployment and therefore same kind of support is delivered from Palo Alto. In this option, it is the responsibility of the customer to manage patches and upgrades of the application. For AWS, Cortex XSOAR publishes an Amazon Machine Image (AMI) that uses Amazon Linux. You can also deploy private-cloud instances of Cortex XSOAR server on GCP or Azure as well.

4) Hybrid Cloud
The hybrid cloud model puts the Cortex XSOAR server in the cloud, either hosted or private, and couples it with a Cortex XSOAR Engine that resides at the central location which is, normally the on-premises server. The Cortex XSOAR Engine allows Cortex XSOAR integrations and automation to talk to on-premises security tools and report back to the Cortex XSOAR Server through the local perimeter. In this model, the customer provisions the image, installs the software, and maintains upgrades and availability while Palo Alto Networks provides the same support as in the on-premises

model. This solution requires to allow HTTPS outbound connections from the Engine to the cloud-based Cortex XSOAR Server.

A minimalist deployment of the Cortex XSOAR platform can be composed of just the XSOAR server alone. And it includes a single app server service and a single database. This single database is considered as the main database, on which all content is stored. The solution architecture and distributed installation options are explained in the next section.

2.2 Software and Hardware Requirements.

The installation of Cortex XSOAR server is supported on the following Operating Systems. You can install the XSOAR application on top of these operating systems. It is also recommended to use a dedicated server to run Cortex XSOAR and not run additional functions or applications on the machine, as it may affect the performance.

Operating System	Supported Versions
CentOS	7.x and 8
Ubuntu	16.04, 18.04, 20.04
RHEL	7.x, 8
Oracle Linux 7.x	7.x
Amazon Linux 2	2

The minimum recommended hardware requirements for Cortex XSOAR server are shown below.

Hardware Requirements	
CPU	16 Cores
Memory	32 GB
Storage	1TB SSD with minimum 3k dedicated IOPS

3. Solution Architecture

3.1 Components of a XSOAR solution

The Cortex XSOAR Server provides a centralized server function for all system operations. The server includes a database that stores incident data. As mentioned earlier, a minimalist deployment of the Cortex XSOAR platform can be composed of just the server alone. Optionally, based on your enterprise size and disaster recovery needs, you may consider to install XSOAR platform in a distributed way to meet scalability and performance requirements.

3.1.1 Cortex XSOAR Engine

Engines are used to expand the operational capacity of a single server by load balancing the integrations and command execution load. Deployment and use of Cortex XSOAR Engines are based on organization's need. The Cortex XSOAR engines are installed in a remote network and allow communication between the remote network and the Cortex XSOAR server. In other words, an Engine acts like a proxy server that enables the local execution of integration-related tasks on isolated protected networks. The Engine initiates all connections for communication with the server, and thus requires only outbound connectivity from the Engine to the server.

3.1.2 Dedicated Database Server

To expand the XSOAR server platform's storage and data-handling capacity, you can deploy one or more dedicated database servers to offload database functions from the main server.
TCP ports 443 and 50001 are used for the database communication.

A dedicated database
server to store the
Incident and Content data

3.1.3 Distributed Database Servers

This multi-tier configuration enables you to scale your XSOAR environment and to manage the resource load. In this, there will be a Main DB server that stores only the content data and the additional DB servers, referred as DB nodes, stores the Incident and incident related data. The content data includes, automations, integrations, playbooks, layouts etc. Incident related data includes, a copy of the playbook used to process the specific incident, indicators extracted from the incident and all the other context data that is created with respect to the incidents.

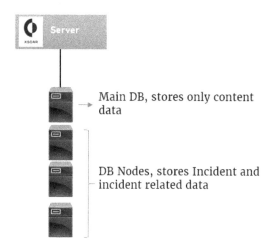

3.1.4 Live backup Server

Live Backup is a high availability option for Cortex XSOAR server. Deployment of a Live Backup server provides an active-passive, manual, failover option for high availability. It enables you to mirror your production server to a backup server, and during any disaster, you can easily convert the backup server to be the production server.

3.1.5 Dev Server

Normally in a production environment, when you want to add or update new contents, it will be fetched from the GitHub repository using the XSOAR marketplace. However, Cortex XSOAR supports the ability to work with separate repositories for development and production environments. This enables the organization to develop and test all of your content in one location, and after the content is finalized, push the content to the remote repository. These remote repositories are Git-Based. Cortex XSOAR content updates are only delivered to the development environment. This enables you to determine which updates you want to push to production. On the production environment, you pull the content and it will be delivered from the Dev-Server.

4. Installing Cortex XSOAR

4.1 Standalone Cortex XSOAR Installation

In this book, I will be illustrating the standalone Cortex XSOAR installation. For testing/practicing purpose, you can request and download the community edition of Cortex XSOAR from Palo Alto website and after reviewing, they will issue a 30 days trial license. The link for installation and the license file will be sent to your mail directly. This link is very important and it is unique for each request.

Follow the link in the mail to download the installer.
Note: For lab purpose, I have used Kali Linux to install and run Cortex XSOAR.

Before proceeding with the installation, let me tell you about Docker. Cortex XSOAR uses Docker to run Python scripts and integrations in a secured, controlled environment. Integrations are run isolated from the server, which prevents accidental damage to the server. While installing XSOAR using the downloaded shell file, it automatically installs Docker, downloads Docker images, and enables remote engine upgrade. Therefore, an internet connectivity is expected.

Note: *There is an offline installation options as well, which includes some manual effort.*
Download the Docker image by appending the parameter **&downloadName=dockerimages** *to the download link you received from Cortex XSOAR. Then copy the downloaded Docker image to the Cortex XSOAR server. Stop the service. Load the Docker image using the command* **sudo docker load -i <YOUR_DOCKER_FILE>.tar**. *Once it is copied, then restart the service.*

Every integration and automation use a Docker image. The image used may be explicitly defined or handled by the system default image, which currently is Python 2.7. The specified Engine for the integration or automation starts the required container and injects into the container the Python code of the integration or automation. Docker will simply run quietly beneath the workflows that analysts use to do their work, without any requirement for intervention. The system makes use of docker engine, which uses docker images to run integrations and automations as containerized applications.

```
root@kali:~/Documents# ./demistoserver-6.0-94597.sh
Verifying archive integrity... All good.
Uncompressing Cortex XSOAR Server Version 6.0-94597 (6.0.2)  100%
Log file: /tmp/demisto_install.log
Installer started with the following flags:
C: false
backup: true
backup-tenants: true
cluster-address:
conffile: /etc/demisto.conf
db-address:
db-any-certificate: true
db-conn-port:
db-node: false
db-only: false
```

Use the downloaded installer to deploy Cortex XSOAR in your server. It will ask you to set the required ports and desired credentials. The default user is **admin** and the default port is **TCP 443**.

```
groupadd: group 'demisto' already exists
Enter server HTTPS port:  (default: '443')
Enter name for admin user:  (default: 'admin')
Enter password for user 'admin':
Password cannot be empty
Enter password for user 'admin': *****
Password must have at least 8 characters
Enter password for user 'admin': ********
Password must have 1 or more uppercase letters
Enter password for user 'admin': ********
Verify password: ********
Server (Secure) Web Port: 443.
Admin user name: `admin`
Are these configurations correct? [yes no] yes
Pulling docker images...
Pulling from demisto/python
Pulling fs layer
```

Once the installation is completed, you can access the Cortex XSOAR web interface using a web browser.
The URL will be **https://<Your-IP-Address>** or by using the localhost.

Installation File Structure

By default, Cortex XSOAR is installed in the /root folder. The file and folder structure in a standard Cortex XSOAR installation is as follows.

Item	Path
Binaries	/usr/local/demisto
Data	/var/lib/demisto
Logs	/var/log/demisto
Configuration	/etc/demisto.conf (will not be created if defaults are selected during installation)
Reports	/tmp/demisto_install.log
Install Log	/tmp/demisto_install.log

Access the URL and login to Cortex XSOAR.

Once you logged in successfully, it will take you to the default Home Page, which is your dashboard. It is recommended to perform a series of tasks to validate the installation, health and the functionality.

4.2. Post-Installation Health check.

After Installing Palo Alto Cortex XSOAR, it is recommended to perform a post-installation health check. As per Palo Alto documentation, the following tests has to be performed.

1) Check the Docker Sub-system

`/docker_images`: Verify that either a list of Docker images or an empty list is returned. You can run this command from the playground.

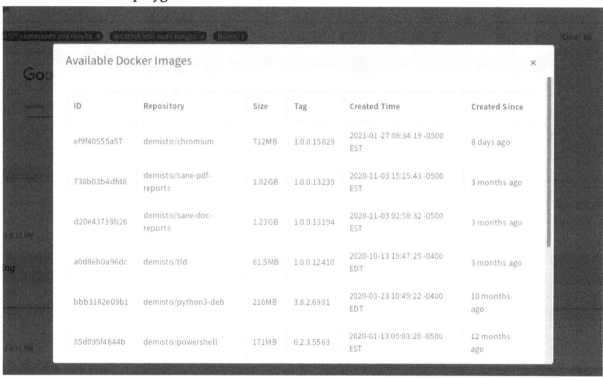

`!py script="demisto.results('hello world')"` : Verify that hello world is returned, if not, there may be issues with your docker installation. You can run this command from the playground.

`sudo docker info`: Run this command from the terminal and Check for warnings or errors.

```
root@kali:~# sudo docker info
Client:
 Context:    default
 Debug Mode: false
 Plugins:
  app: Docker App (Docker Inc., v0.9.1-beta3)
  buildx: Build with BuildKit (Docker Inc., v0.5.1-docker)

Server:
 Containers: 13
  Running: 12
  Paused: 0
  Stopped: 1
 Images: 16
 Server Version: 20.10.3
 Storage Driver: overlay2
  Backing Filesystem: extfs
  Supports d type: true
```

2) Verify Integration Tests

Create an instance of each of the following integrations and test each of these integrations by clicking the Test button in the integration instance. You can also optionally run associated commands in the playground. Sample integration installation of **ipinfo** is shown below.

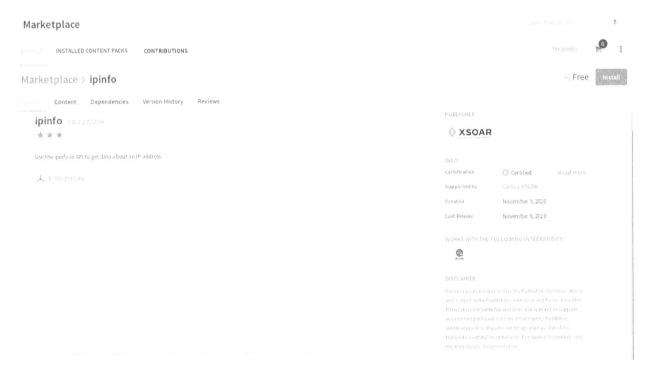

- urlscan.io
- ipinfo
- PhishTank

- OpenPhish
- Rasterize

Also, run **!FailedInstances** in the playground to test all configured integrations and check outputs to validate that there are no errors returned.

3) Run Commands in the Playground.

Note that if the above-mentioned integrations are not done, then the following commands cannot be executed. Means the commands are imported in to the system with the installation of the integrations.

`!url url=https://google.com` : Check for URL reputation.

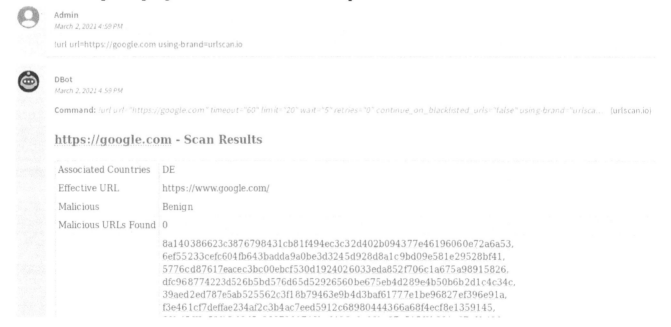

`!ip ip="8.8.8.8"` : This check for the reputation of the IP address

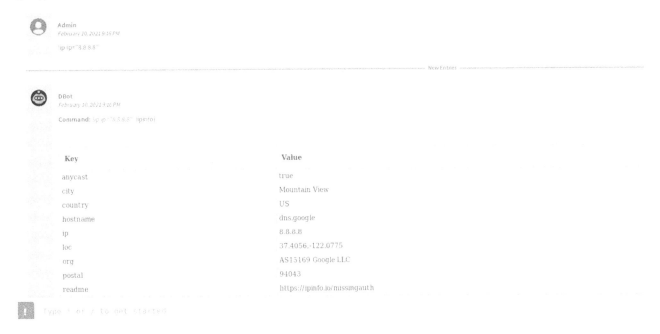

`!rasterize url="https://google.com"`
`!rasterize-email htmlBody="<h1>hello world</h1>"`
Converts the contents of a URL/Email to an image file or a PDF file.

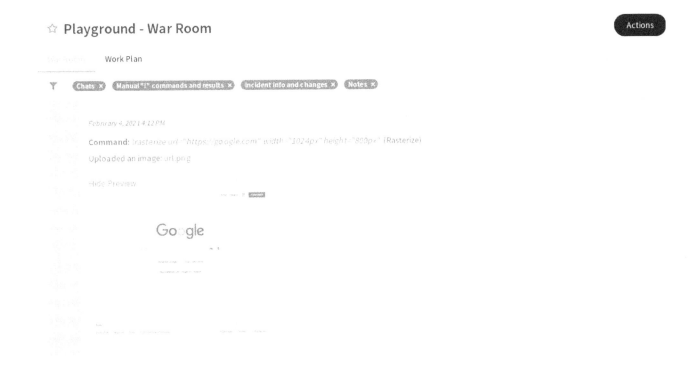

Verify the internet connectivity by using `!Ping address=8.8.8.8`

Ping.

5) Run any report and verify that the PDF output resolves correctly.

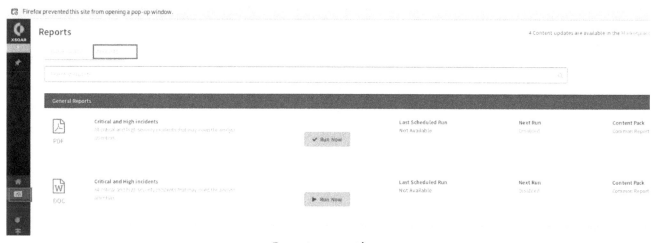

Report generation.

6) Verify that you see automation scripts in the Automation section.

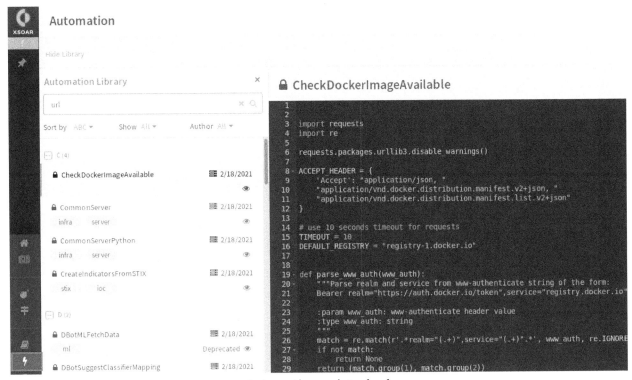

Automation scripts check.

7) Verify that you see playbooks in the Playbooks section.

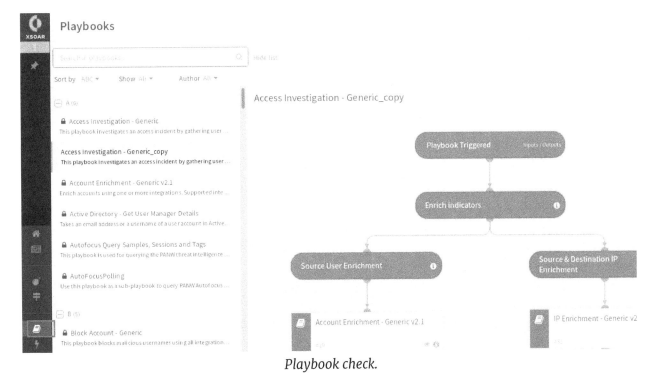

Playbook check.

7) Verify that you see dashboard widgets in the My Dashboards section.

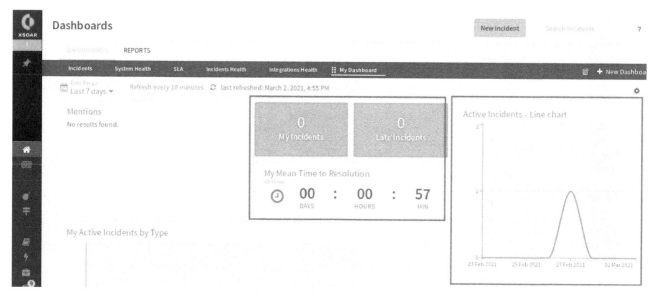

dashboard widgets check.

5. Basic Configurations

So far, we have successfully installed the Cortex XSOAR and verified the installation by performing the post-installation health check. Now, let's configure the Cortex XSOAR server with some basic settings.

5.1 Adding Mail-Sender Integration

Mail-Sender integration is used to send mails from XSOAR server to the outside world. For example, if you want to invite a user, or to send incident reminders to the analysts, a mail-sender integration is necessary. There is a separate chapter on Integration and marketplace, where I explained things in detail.

Mail Sender integration is installed by default with Cortex XSOAR Installation. But if you cannot find it under integrations, you can always go to the Marketplace and install the integration.

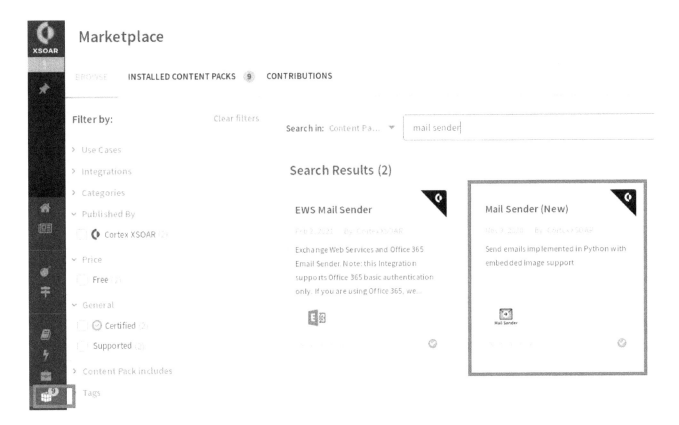

To setup the Mail Sender integration, Navigate to **Settings > Integrations** and search for **Mail Sender**

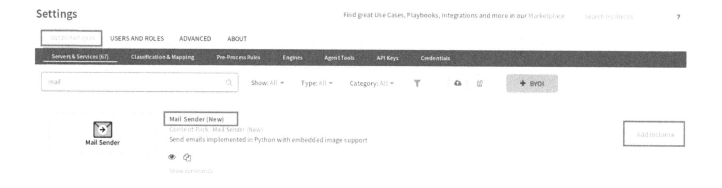

Click on Add instance.

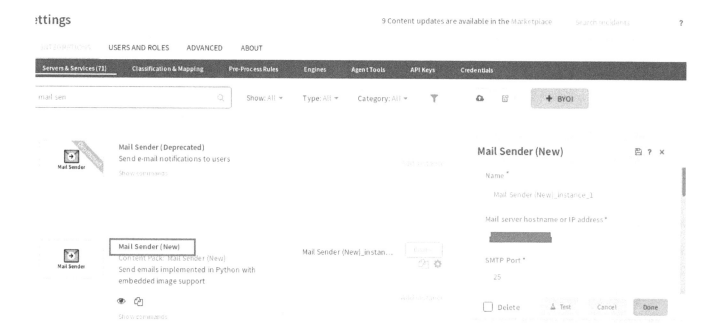

In the configuration window, specify a name for the Integration instance. You can give any desired name. Then mention the Mail server IP address and in the SMTP port field, provide the Port details. Here I set the default instance name.

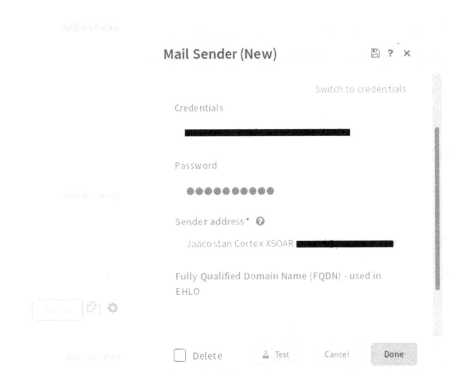

Mention your credential details and the sender address. The mails will be sent with the mentioned sender address.

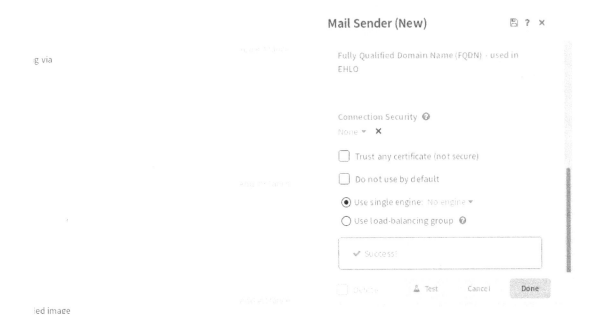

Name, Mail server IP, Port, credentials and the sender address are the mandatory fields. Then click on test button. This will validate whether the mentioned details are valid or not. If valid, it will show a Success banner. Then click on Done.

Now the integration instance has been created successfully. If you want to change any settings, you can always click on the settings (gear icon) next to the instance.

5.2 Adding Users in to Cortex XSOAR

Cortex XSOAR supports local as well as external authentication methods. Means you can add users locally or by integrating external identity sources like Active Directory, LDAP etc. Before explaining the authentication using the external sources, lets learn how to add additional users in the Cortex XSOAR server.

To add a user, navigate to Settings > Users and Roles > Users

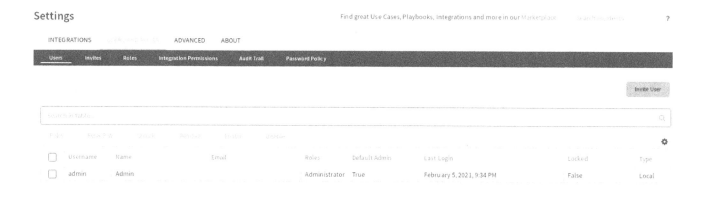

Here on the **Users** page, you can see the default administrator "admin".

Adding a new user in XSOAR is done by invitations. Basically, you invite a user by providing their email address, the user will receive the mail and the person can activate his account by following the link received in the mail.

Click on **Invite User**

Provide the email address of the user that you want to add and assign a role. We will be discussing more on Roles in the following sections.

Then click on Invite button. Since we have already configured the Mail-Sender integration, the invitation mail will be sent to the user by XSOAR.

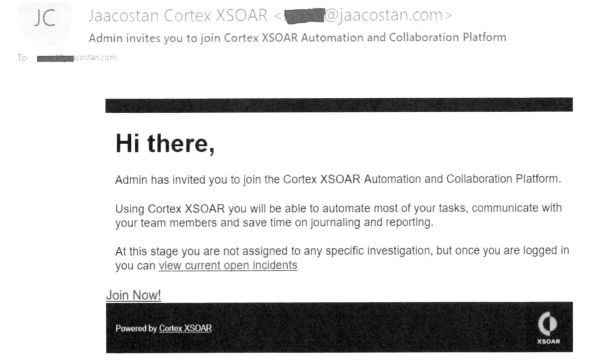

The user will receive the mail instantly. You can see the sender address which we mentioned earlier in the mail-sender integration settings.

The User now just need to click on "Join Now!" to accept the invite and to set the credentials. The link will be opened on a web browser.

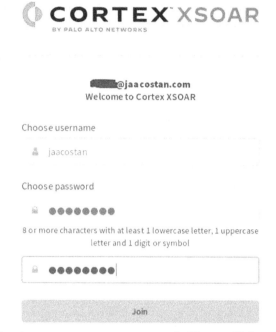

Choose a desired username and set your account password. Then Click Join to complete the process and it will take you to the default dashboard page. Note that, once the username is set, you cannot change it. You can further customize your profile from Cortex XSOAR.

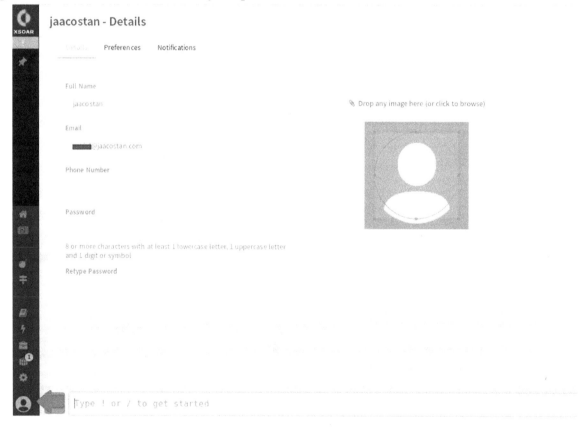

Click on the current user (icon at the extreme bottom left.) and it will show your profile page.
Here you can change your name, email address, password and photo. Note that, changing your full name won't change your Username. The Username that you set during the invitation signup is permanent.

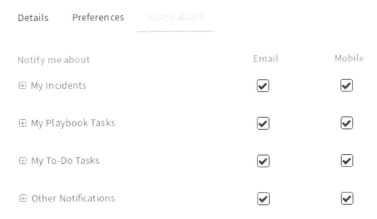

You can also configure the notification settings and the delivery options from the Notification menu. Now, what if the Mail-Sender Integration is not set? Well, to add a new user, Mail-Sender integration is not mandatory. Same process, you send an invitation to the user. But the mail will not be delivered.

You can see the user invite under the Invites tab. Copy the invite URL and open it on a new browser window. It will give the same signup page, where you can provide the username and set the password.

Also note, the **Accepted** field. When the user accepts the invitation by clicking the link, then the field status will change to true.

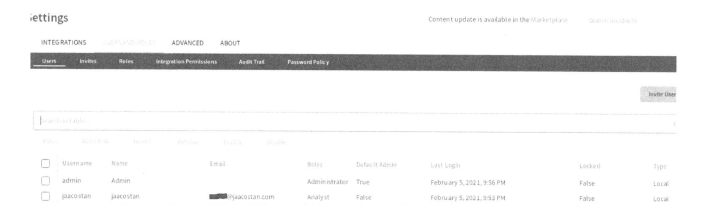

The new user has been successfully added to the Cortex XSOAR with the assigned role.

5.3 External Authentication

To map network accounts or to authenticate users with external sources like Active Directory, LDAP, SAML, Duo etc., we need to configure the required integration first.

In this example, I am setting up an Active Directory based authentication method. You can install the desired integration from the marketplace. Once the Integration is installed, go to **Settings > Integrations > Servers and Services** to create an integration instance.

Locate or search for the Integration "Active Directory Authentication"

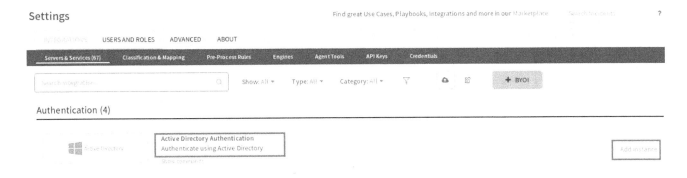

Click on **Add instance.**

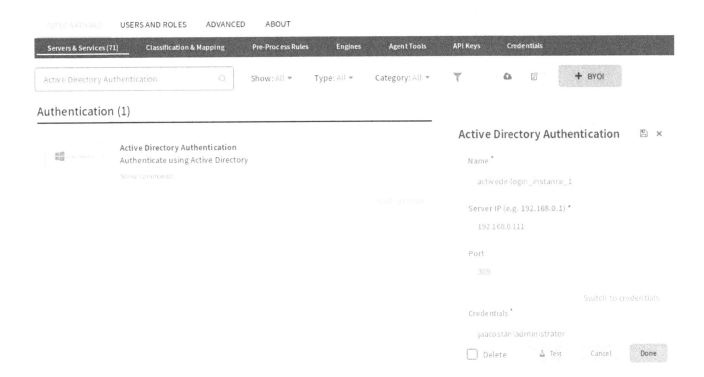

Provide a name for the integration instance, then mention the IP address of the AD server and the port. Also mention the credentials to authenticate with AD.

Provide the Base DN. In my case, I have setup an Organization Unit (OU) in my AD named as **SOC_Admins**. So, the Base DN is **OU=SOC_Admins, DC=jaacostan, DC=local**.

If you have implemented security for your AD, you can select that as well from the Security Type dropdown menu. I don't have, so I selected none.

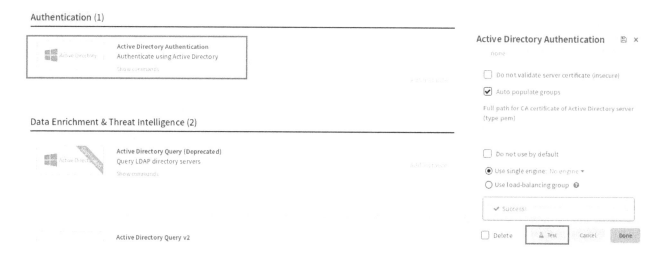

Then Click on Test to validate the settings. Once it is shown as success, click on Done and the integration instance has been created.

For the authentication purpose, the AD role mapping has to be configured from the **Settings > Users and Roles > Roles** tab.

You can map the AD to the existing roles, but for the illustration purpose, I will create a new role names "SOC_Analyst_AD"

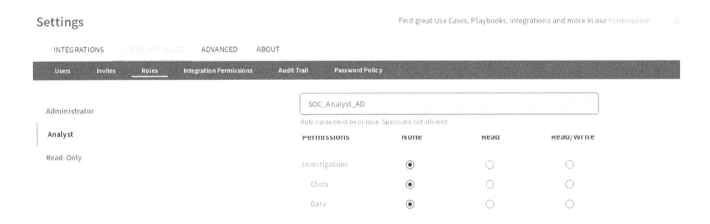

You can set some permissions for the new roles.

Don't get confused about the roles for now, the next section is about Role Based Access Control, where I have mentioned each and every role setting.

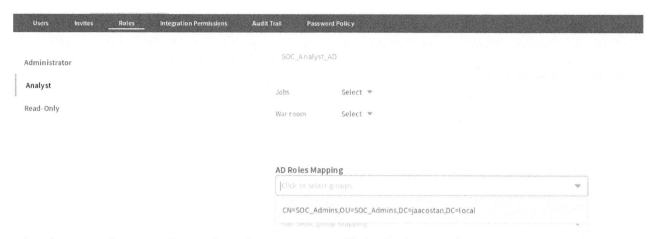

Under the AD roles mapping, select the group. It will fetch the details through the AD integration instance, which we have configured in the previous section.

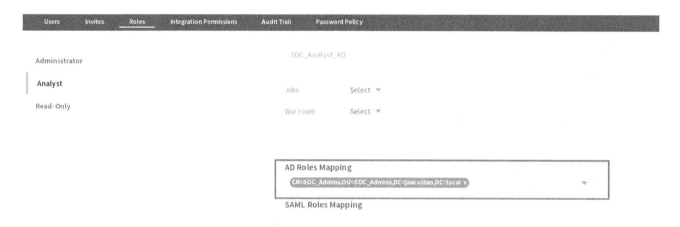

Map the role and then click on Save.

You can view the newly created role under the Roles Tab.

Now we need to test this. Before that I will show you the user group from the Active Directory Server.

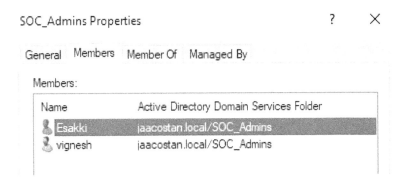

I have two users in the group. Both will be able to login in to XSOAR using their Active Directory Credentials. Means, if a role is mapped to an AD group, all the users in that group will be able to log in to the Cortex XSOAR server. Once they logged in to XSOAR for the first time, they will automatically get listed under the Users page as well.

Let's test this with an AD user "Vignesh". Go to the login page of Cortex XSOAR. The user can login to the system using NTLM or by using the UPN format.

A successful login will take you to the user's default dashboard page.

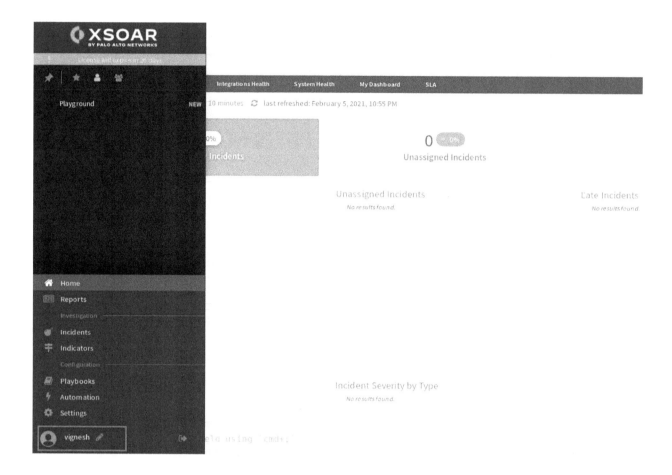

I haven't assigned much privileges to this particular user. Let's login as admin and verify the Users page. Under **Users and Roles > Users**, you can now see the new user "Vignesh".

Also note the type option. It will show the user type, here in this case the user is authenticated using Active Directory and therefore shown the type as AD.

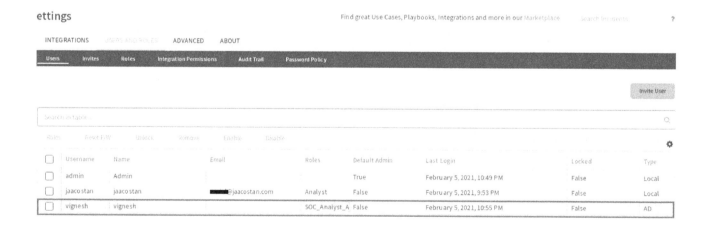

Username	Name	Email	Roles	Default Admin	Last Login	Locked	Type
admin	Admin			True	February 5, 2021, 10:49 PM	False	Local
jaacostan	jaacostan	▓@jaacostan.com	Analyst	False	February 5, 2021, 9:53 PM	False	Local
vignesh	vignesh		SOC_Analyst_A	False	February 5, 2021, 10:55 PM	False	AD

5.4 Role Based Access Control

By default, besides the Default Admin, Cortex XSOAR has 3 out of the box roles. Administrator, Analyst and Read-Only. It is also possible to create additional roles with granular access controls. Administrator Role has read/write permission to all components and access to all pages. Analyst role is a role with mixed privileges. They don't need write access to certain integrations or they don't need privileges to add users or create playbooks. Read-Only roles provides users with only the read access to all the pages.

Lets create a role and go through the permission options.

While creating a role, you can define the permissions to Investigation Chats and Data. There is a checkbox saying "This role can execute potential harmful actions". Checking this box enables the users to execute the defined potential commands. Potentially harmful commands are those, that could cause loss of data, network changes, weaken the security, etc if incorrectly or improperly used. A single integration may support many commands. Several out-of-the-box integrations include some commands that Palo Alto Networks has marked as Potentially harmful as the default setting.

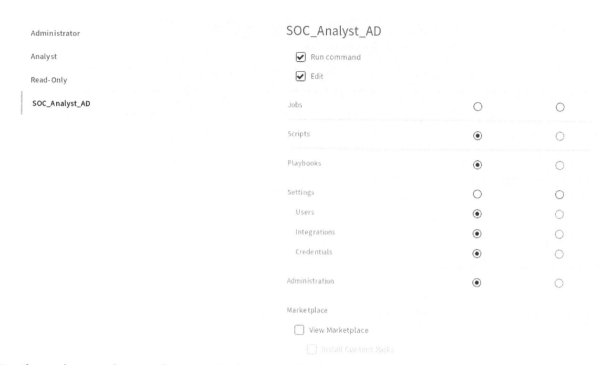

Further give read or write permissions to the important XSOAR contents such as Scripts, Jobs, Playbooks , access to Marketplace etc.

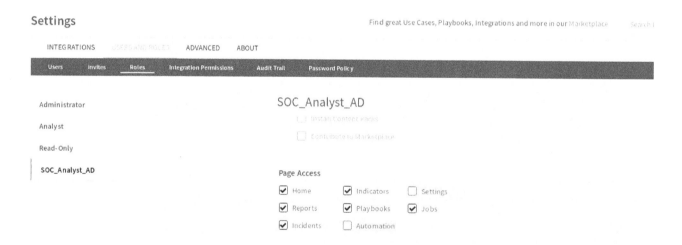

Role-based options also control access to editing privileges for Jobs, Scripts, Playbooks, Settings, and Administration features. For each role, you also can control access to top-level pages, which are Home, Reports, Incidents, Indicators, Playbooks, Automation, Settings, and Jobs. If you have given permission to access investigation data but didn't give the privilege to access the page, then the user won't be able to use his permissions.

For this particular SOC_Analyst_AD role, I have denied the access to the Automation and Settings Page.

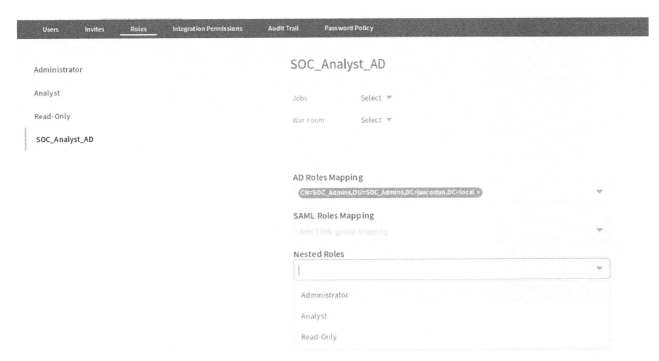

Another option is to add Nested Roles. Nested roles are roles added to an existing role. This can be useful when you want to give some extra privileges to an existing role.

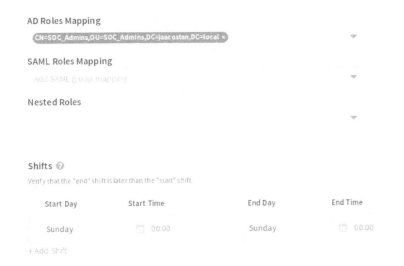

Shift management helps you define multiple shifts within Cortex XSOAR. Each shift can be assigned to a user role so you are able to assign one or more analysts across different shifts. After assigning the role to users, Cortex XSOAR recommends to whom the incident can be assigned. While assigning an analyst to an incident, these shifts can be taken into account.

Once the necessary privileges are set, click on save and now the role has been successfully created.

Lets login with the new role. Since the role is mapped with AD user group, I will use the user "vignesh" to login to verify the RBAC permissions.

The user "Vignesh" don't have the access to the Settings and Automation pages and hence it is not listed Menu.

In case the admin want to change the role of an existing user, it can be easily achieved from the Users page. Select the user and edit the role assigned. It is also possible to add multiple roles to the same user.

In order to make a user as the default admin, they first need to be assigned to the Administrator role. To assign a user as the default admin, select a user assigned to the Admin role, click the Roles button and select the Set as Default Admin checkbox.

6. Familiarize with Cortex XSOAR GUI

Let's get familiarize with the Web interface of Cortex XSOAR. This is just a brief walkthrough of the Cortex XSOAR GUI and consider this as an introduction of Cortex XSOAR web interface. The important settings and features are comprehensively explained in the remaining sections of this book.

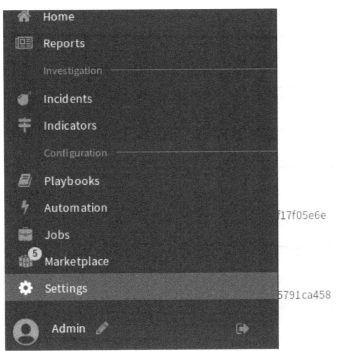

6.1 Settings

All the main components, configurations are done from the settings page. Here you can create the integration instances, create the roles and users, create incident and indicator types, layouts, classification and mapping, advanced server configurations, backup etc.

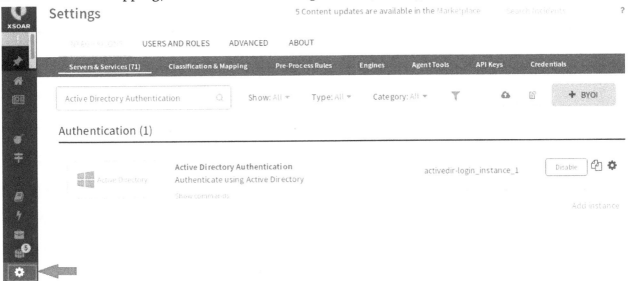

The first tab is the Integration tab. All the integrations that we installed from the market place will be available user settings > Servers and Services tab. Another option is Classification and Mapping. This is where we define the incident classification, mapping of incident and indicator fields. You can add advanced features such as adding engines, storing credentials etc. from the same Servers&Services page.

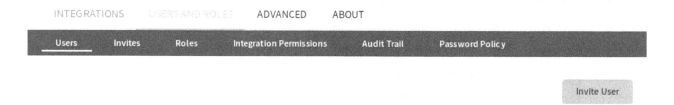

The second tab is Users and Roles. Here you can Add users, set permissions, view audit trial, set the password policy etc.

The third tab is Advanced. Here you can create new incident fields, Incident and indicator types, create and manage the layouts, create lists, configure backup and create ML models. Each incident has a layout, an incident type and multiple fields.

The last tab is the About page. Here you can manage and view your licenses, and from the Troubleshooting page, you can download the logs, export/import contents and add various server and database parameters.

6.2 Marketplace

Cortex XSOAR Marketplace is the central location for installing, exchanging, contributing, and managing all of your content, including playbooks, integrations, automations, fields, layouts, and more. If you are a developer, you can upload content and view your contributions. The authors of the integrations release new updates for the existing integrations and the update can be also performed from the Marketplace. And in any case, if you want to uninstall any integration from the Cortex XSOAR server, that also can be done from the Marketplace.

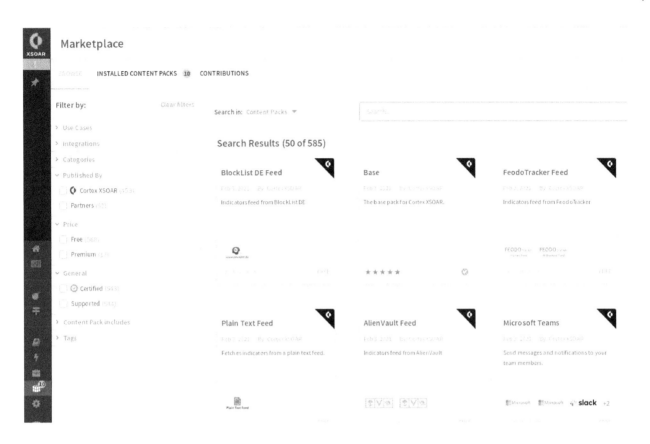

All content on Marketplace is included in a Content Pack which is digitally signed and it can be free or paid (premium). A Content Pack is like a small content repository, and it contains all relevant content items under its directories. A content pack includes,

- Classifiers
- Dashboard Widgets and Reports
- Incident Fields and Incident Types
- Indicator Fields and Indicator Types
- Layouts (Incident and Indicator Layouts)
- Playbooks
- Scripted Automations
- Technology Integrations

6.3 Automations.

Automation page lists all the automation scripts available in your XSOAR server where you manage, create, and modify scripts. You can use these automations in playbook tasks to achieve the desired goal. These scripts perform a specific action, and are comprised of commands associated with an integration. You can write scripts in Python, PowerShell and in JavaScript. Scripts can access all Cortex XSOAR APIs, access to incidents, investigations and share data to the War Room. You can also create your own automations from this page. The Automation page also includes a Script Helper, which provides a list of available commands and scripts, ordered alphabetically.

6.4 Integrations.

Cortex XSOAR integrations are blocks of code that connect Cortex XSOAR to external systems and services by use of standard APIs and they are the foundational components of the Cortex XSOAR security orchestration, automation, and response capability. Integrations provide runtime functions that generate incidents and commands that can be called from within the context of a specific incident.

You add and extend the functionalities of Cortex XSOAR by adding the integrations. Without integrations, Cortex XSOAR is just an application with not input and outputs.

The integrations in XSOAR can be categorized into four main types.

1) System Admin

   The integrations which fall under this category are used for the add the system related functions such as external authentications, mail sender or listener, integration with external messaging systems, directory lookups or MFA integration etc.

2) Event Ingestion

   These types of integrations are used to fetch events and alerts from the external systems such as SIEM tools, Syslog, monitoring tools etc. The incidents in XSOAR are normally created with the help of Event ingestion Integration

3) Enrichment

When an alert is ingested and an incident is created, various information including URLs, IP addresses, and files can be extracted from the raw incident data. XSOAR can check the extracted data against your organization's available threat-intelligence services by running playbook tasks that execute commands that are associated with additional integrations. For example, if you want to verify the reputation of an IP mentioned in the incident, then the integrations that falls under the enrichment category can be used.

4) Response and Remediation

Cortex XSOAR can automatically respond to an incident and can remediate by communicating with the different tools deployed in your environment. For example, if a virus was detected, XSOAR can automatically inform the Endpoint security solution to isolate the device and to perform scan. Also, it can communicate with firewall to block any particular IP or port associated with the malware. These automated orchestrations can be done by adding the necessary integrations.

Let's illustrate the installation and instance configuration using a demo. For this I will use the Active Directory Query Integration. Active Directory Query integration enables you to access and manage Active Directory objects (users, contacts, and computers). Integrations are usually included in the content pack.

First go to the marketplace to install the required content packs.

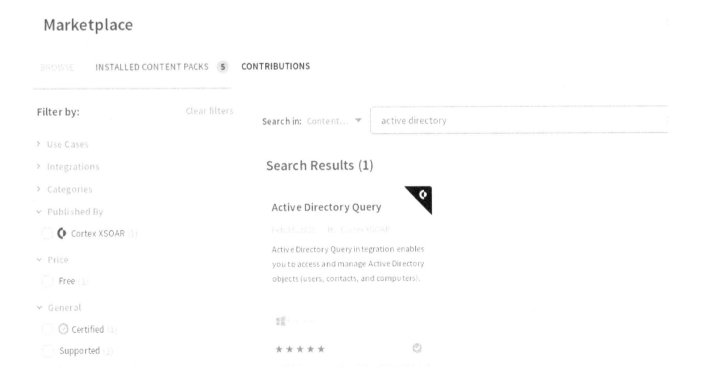

Click on the "Active Directory Query" content pack and install it. You can also view what are the details included with this Content pack.

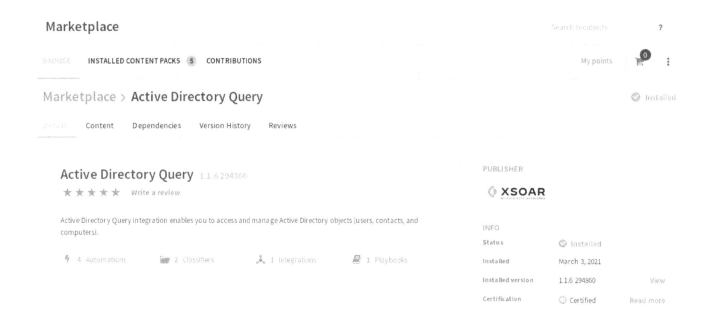

There are 4 automations, classifiers, 1 Integrations and 1 Playbook, which are automatically installed with this integration. Once installed successfully, next is to configure the integration Instance. Navigate to **Settings > Integrations > Servers & Services**, and search for **Active Directory Query**.

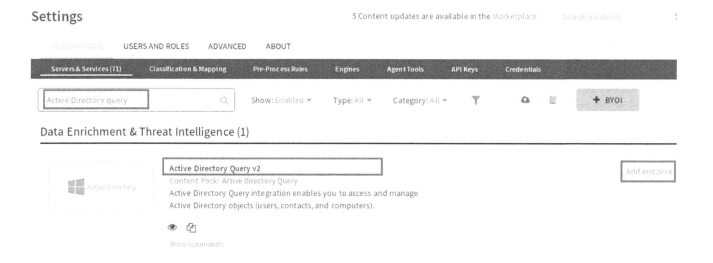

Click on Add instance.

In the configuration popup window, give a name for the integration instance, mention your Active Directory Server IP address.

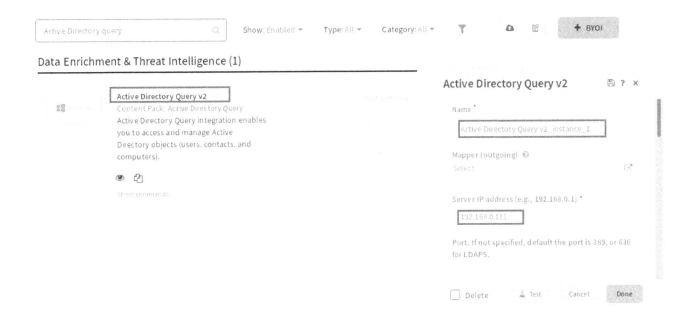

Provide your domain credentials to authenticate with AD server.

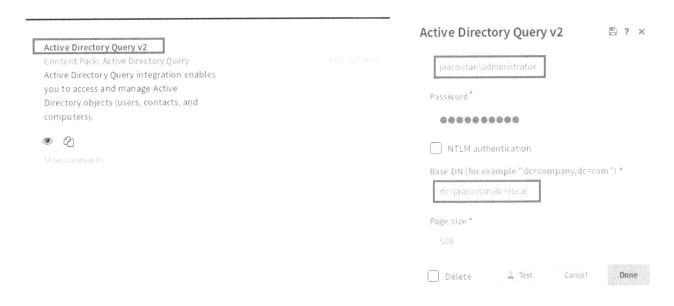

Mention the Base DN. In my case, dc=jaacostan, dc=local.

Leave remaining options as default and click on Test. If the configuration is valid, it will show the success banner. Then click Done.

Now you can see the integration instance under the Active Directory Query v2 instance.

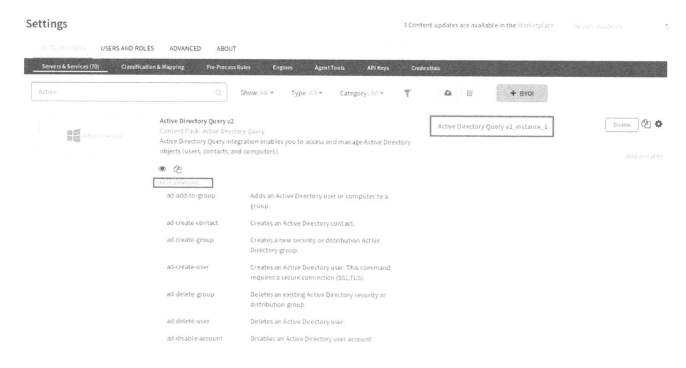

Each integration supports a lot of commands. So, when an instance is configured, these commands are also get added in to the XSOAR system. To view the commands supported by the specific instance, you can click on show commands. For this particular instance, you can see commands like ad-add-to-group, ad-create-contact etc.

You can issue these commands from the Command line interface option in the XSOAR GUI. Once issued, the commands will run in the playground, which is a test ground in the XSOAR server to do your testing.

Let's do some testing. Search for the details of an AD user "Esakki" by executing the following command.

!ad-get-user username="Esakki"

Please note that, this command will work only if we have already installed the required integrations and configured with the instances.

Active Directory - Get Users

displayName	Esakki
dn	CN=Esakki,OU=SOC_Admins,DC=jaacostan,DC=local
mail	
manager	
memberOf	CN=SOC_Admins,OU=SOC_Admins,DC=jaacostan,DC=local
name	Esakki
sAMAccountName	esakki
userAccountControl	512

The integration will run in the background and fetch the information from the Active Directory. What about adding a new user in to the AD? Let's do it.

Create a user named "bob" using the **!ad-create-user** command

```
!ad-create-user username="bob" password="P@ssw0rdforBob" user-
dn="CN=bob,OU=SOC_Admins,DC=jaacostan,DC=local" display-name="bob" description="Created by
XSOAR" title="Analyst"
```

Now verify the details from the AD server.

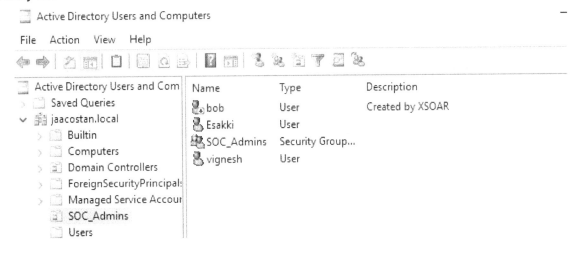

We can see that the user has been created successfully.

Though I used this integration instance to demonstrate some of the features, now imagine the usage in a complex scenario. You can make use of multiple different instances and integrations to achieve a particular task or goal within seconds. That is what playbooks do. It automates different tasks with the use of integrations to meet the objectives.

6.5 XSOAR commands

So, we have seen some unfamiliar commands. Let' talk about the scripts and commands in Cortex XSOAR.

External/Integrations commands

Along with integrations, we get some integration commands and scripts. They are executed by using an exclamation mark (!) as prefix. Integration commands are also known as external commands. In the above example, we installed the Active Directory Query v2 integration, and used those integrations commands to perform some functions. Some integration comes with some automation scripts as well. These scripts perform specific actions and comprise commands associated with an integration object.

The above image shows an example for using external commands. Note that all the integration or external commands begins with small letter case. Not let's see about external scripts.

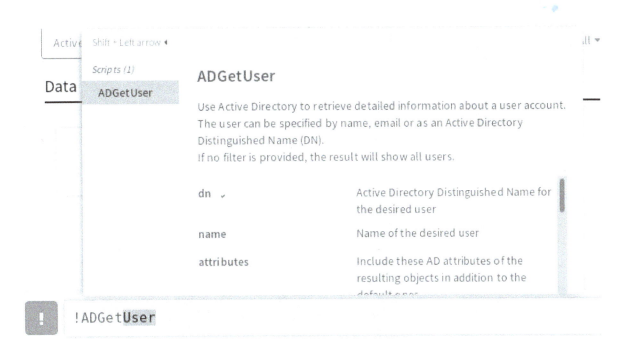

Scripts begins with Upper case letter. All the external scripts and commands are used with an exclamation (!) prefix.

System Commands.

Commands that enable you to perform some specific Cortex XSOAR operations related to the systems, incident operations and other system related tasks such as clearing playgrounds, managing docker related tasks etc. These commands are not specific to an integration. System commands are entered in the command line using a forward slash mark (/) prefix, for example, /incident_add.

Let's install another integration instance. VirusTotal. Virus total is used to analyze suspicious hashes, URLs, domains and IP addresses. When an incident is created, XSOAR can extract all the identified indicators from the incident information and with the help of integrations like VirusTotal, the analyst can get instant details of the indicators and its reputation.

To install the integration, as always, go to the Marketplace.

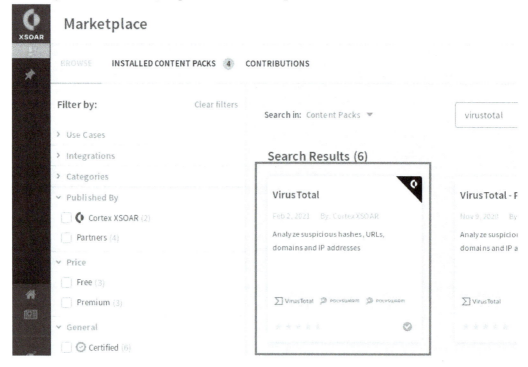

Install the Content Pack.

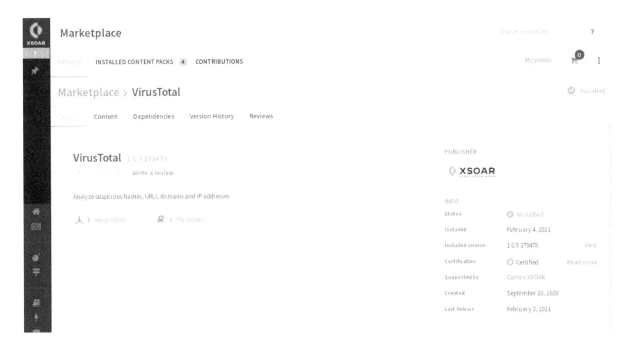

Now go to the Integrations page (Settings > Servers & Services) and access the VirusTotal Integrations.

An integration is useless unless you create an instance of it. Let's create an instance. Click on Add instance.

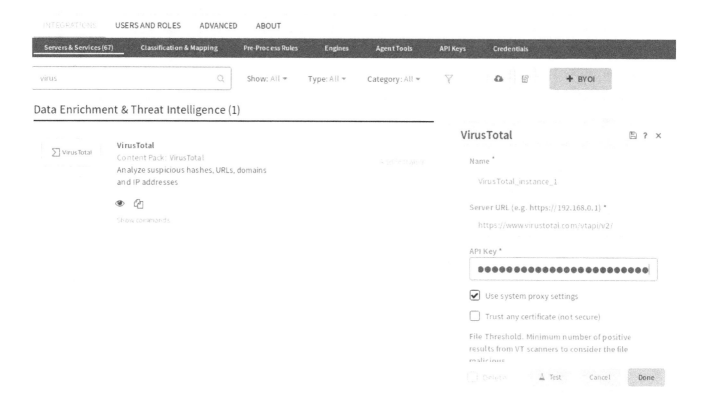

Configure the instance. Specify a name, server URL and an API key. You can sign up for a free account and get an API key from VirusTotal website.

Test the integration and it should return success. Click Done.
Now you have successfully created an instance of the VirusTotal Integration.

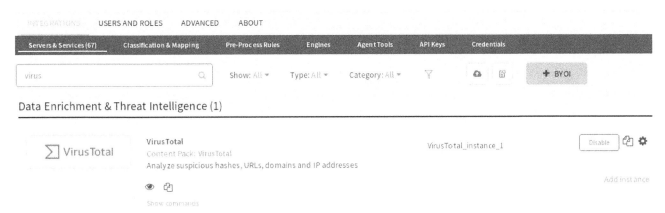

You can see the commands supported by the VirusTotal Integration.

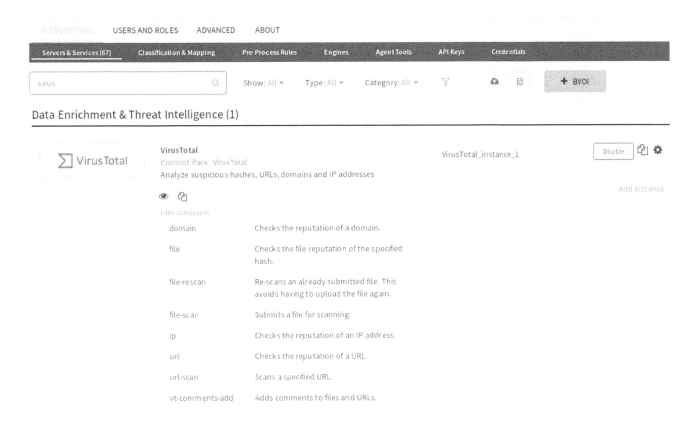

Means, you can use these commands for your incident investigations. Also, you can disable the instance as well. Disabling an Integration instance will not remove any external commands from the XSOAR system; however, you won't be able to use it unless you have an active integration instance.

Go through the VirusTotal integration commands.

There are multiple integrations available that provide same features. For example, an IP reputation can be checked by using VirusTotal as well as ipinfo integration. The **ip** command is supported by both Integrations. So, you can use "using=" argument to select a particular instance.

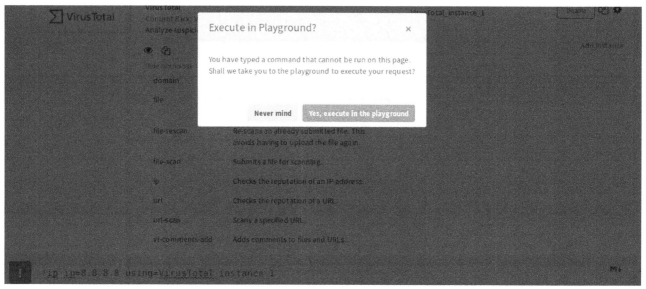

You can execute the commands from different XSOAR pages; It will run in the background and you can access the results from the Playground.

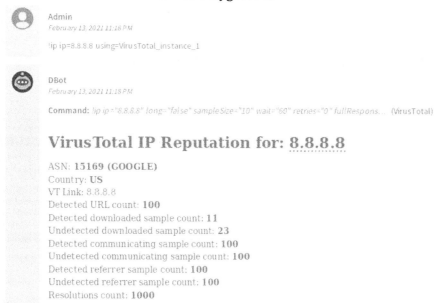

Admin
February 13, 2021 11:18 PM

!ip ip=8.8.8.8 using=VirusTotal_instance_1

DBot
February 13, 2021 11:18 PM

Command: !ip ip="8.8.8.8" long="false" sampleSize="10" wait="60" retries="0" fullRespons... (VirusTotal)

VirusTotal IP Reputation for: 8.8.8.8

ASN: **15169 (GOOGLE)**
Country: **US**
VT Link: 8.8.8.8
Detected URL count: **100**
Detected downloaded sample count: **11**
Undetected downloaded sample count: **23**
Detected communicating sample count: **100**
Undetected communicating sample count: **100**
Detected referrer sample count: **100**
Undetected referrer sample count: **100**
Resolutions count: **1000**

It will run instantly and gives the result to the analyst. An internet connectivity is expected for querying with intelligence sources in the internet and thereby returning the results.

6.6 Incidents

You can view and manage all your pending, active and closed incidents from the incidents page.

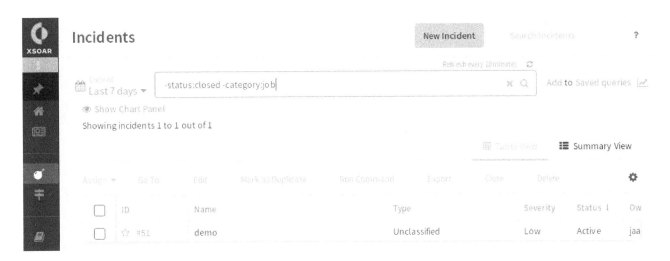

You can do various incident management actions such as assigning the incident to an analyst, delete, close, export etc. You can also set the view. There are three customizable viewing options. Chart, table view and Summary view.

The incidents are searchable and you can use the Lucene Query language to perform the search query. In the above image, the search query is **–status:closed –category:job.**

The hyphen (–) functions as a NOT operator. **–status:closed** means, the incidents that are not closed. Similarly **–category:job** means, the incident category not equals a job. These are two different queries put together with a space. Here the query executes with an OR operator. When you execute the above query, XSOAR will list all the incidents with –status:closed **or** –category:job. You can also use the "**and**" operator to filter your queries.

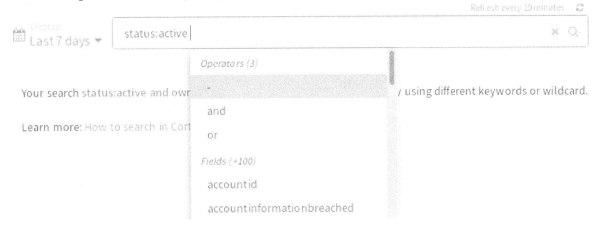

One important thing here to note is, the search queries are Case sensitive and all are in small case.

6.7 Indicators

The Indicators page displays all indicators discovered and are available in your XSOAR server, and enables you to perform several indicator actions. You can also select one or more indicators and create an incident directly from the Indicators page. Indicators are artifacts associated with incidents, and are an essential part of the incident management and remediation process. They help to correlate incidents, create hunting operations, and enable you to easily analyze incidents and reduce the Mean Time To Resolve (MTTR).

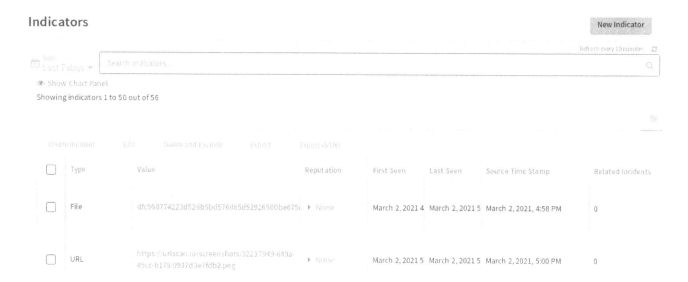

Indicators are detected and ingested to Cortex XSOAR through integrations such as feeds, mail etc., from Incidents using the manual or auto extraction, Regex query, scripts or by uploading the STIX file.

6.8 Reports and Dashboards

The XSOAR dashboard consists of visualized data using customizable widgets, which enables you to analyze data from inside or outside Cortex XSOAR, in different formats such as graphs, pie charts, or text. You can customize what information you want to view and set a time period as well. The widgets in the dashboard can be resized to customize the layout. Further you can share the dashboard created by you with other Cortex XSOAR users.

By default, Cortex XSOAR is installed with a default dashboard with the following tabs.
Incidents: information relating to incidents, such as severity type, active incidents, unassigned incidents etc.

System Health: information relating to the Cortex XSOAR Server health such as CPU usage, Disk/Memory usage etc.

My Dashboard: a personalized dashboard relating to your incidents, tasks, and so on.

SLA: information relating to your Service Level Agreement.

Incident Health: Status of incident progress such as failed incidents, errors, etc.

Integration Health: Shows the status of the Integrations. If any of the integrations are not working or having errors, it will display the information here.

You can create new incident manually from the Dashboards page directly.

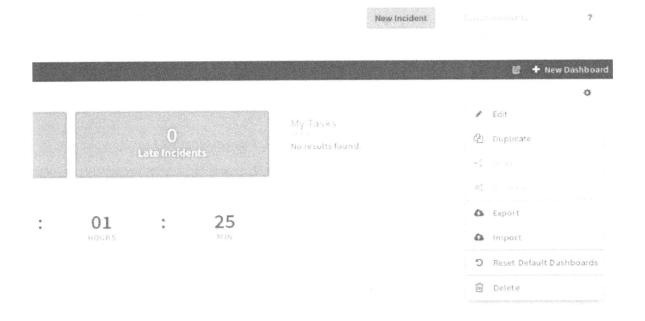

Click on the gear icon to edit your dashboard. You can also duplicate, share, import, export, delete dashboard as well.

When you edit your dashboard, you can customize the widgets, add/remove widgets as per your requirements.

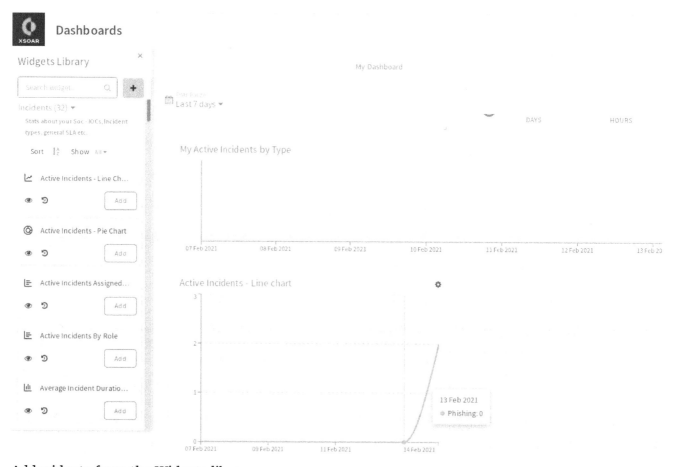

Add widgets from the Widgets library.

After making the changes, save the dashboard. As best practice, it is always recommended to use save version. This enables the change log and makes roll back easy.

Reports contain statistical data information which enables you create reports in PDF, Word and CSV formats. A report also contains widgets, which enables you to analyze data from Cortex XSOAR, in different formats such as graphs, pie charts, or text. Cortex XSOAR comes with out-of-the-box reports, such as critical and High incidents, Daily incidents, last 7 days incidents, etc. These reports cannot be edited except the schedule time and who can receive the report.

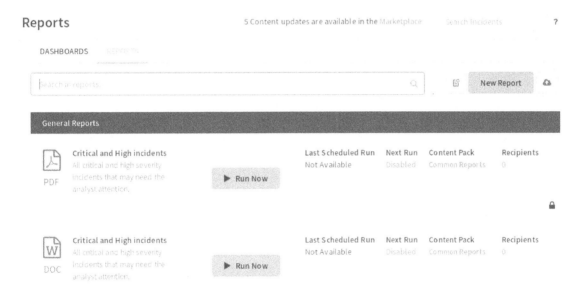

6.9 Jobs

You can create scheduled events/tasks in Cortex XSOAR using jobs. Jobs are triggered either by time-triggered events or feed-triggered events. You can schedule jobs to fetch new indicators from Threat Intel feeds. Or you can create a job to remove the expired indicators. A playbook can be attached to perform the automated tasks and gets triggered based on the Job criteria.

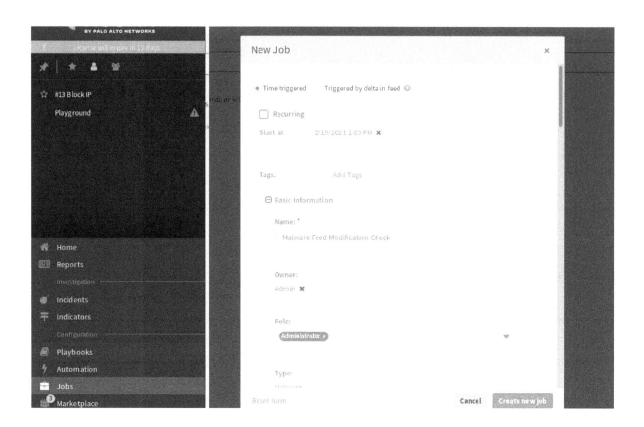

7. Incident Management Lifecycle in Cortex XSOAR

We all know about the incident management and response process and the responsibilities of a SOC. It includes the planning, identifying an incident, Investigate, mitigate and the continues improvement of process and tools. Cortex XSOAR helps to orchestrate and automate the entire process using playbooks and by integrating with various tools available in your organization.

When your organization deploy the Cortex XSOAR solution, there are a lot of tasks and configurations that has to be done to make the XSOAR system active and ready. It is important to ask a few questions to yourself before configuring the tool. For example,

- Why are we using this XSOAR tool?
- Which incident investigations has to be automated? Identify the use cases such as Phishing Incidents, Malware incidents etc. related to your environment and needs.
- What are the available tools that has to be integrated with the XSOAR system?

Based on this, you have to initiate your planning, followed with the process configuration. In other words, the organization might already have an Incident Response Standard Operating Procedure (SOP) or runbook for each kind of incidents. Now with Cortex XSOAR, we can automate the entire process and procedure with the help of Playbooks.

The steps to configure your Cortex XSOAR from a fresh perspective are explained in this section. It involves a lot of planning and effort to achieve the desired goal.

Note: For an easy understanding, the entire incident lifecycle in XSOAR will be explained using a custom incident related to Spam mails.

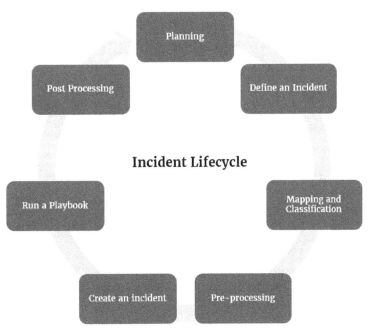

The logical steps involved with each phase of the incident lifecycle are summarized in the below flow chart. Follow the chapters and sections in the order (without skipping) to understand the flow correctly.

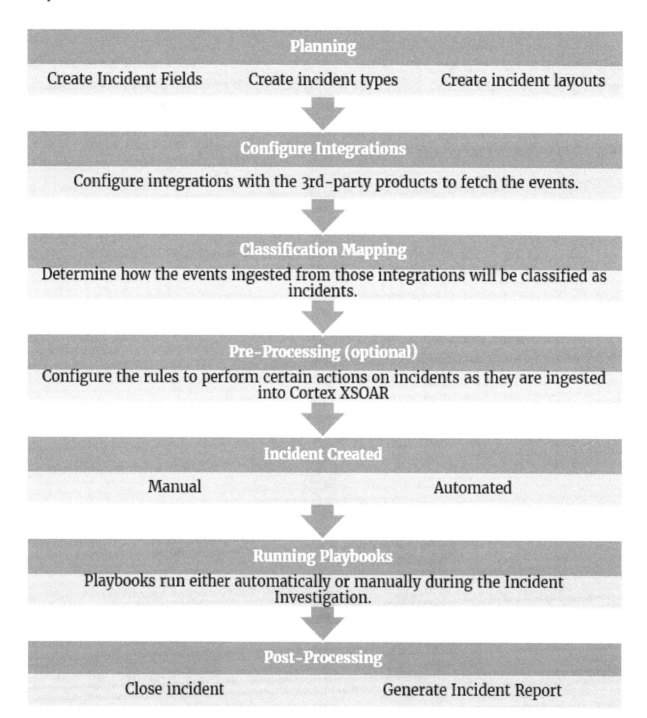

7.1 Planning

You perform the planning with a particular Incident type in your mind. To create and handle the incident, you have to integrate with various third-party tools and solutions. You also need to plan how the events are ingested from the third-party tools by Cortex XSOAR, how the incident has to be displayed to the analysts, what should be the layout, is it required to create any additional field to map the incident data etc. The answers to all these questions have to be gathered during this planning phase.

For the illustration purpose, I want to automate the investigation of incidents related to Spam Mail. Let's assume that the users in the organization receives spam mails and some mails might be malicious and risky to the user as well. It is good to gather some basic information related to the incident during this planning phase. Such as,

1) How the events/alerts are detected and ingested to XSOAR.? Which integration I need to use for getting the event data related to spam mails?
2) Is there an Incident type for spam mail investigation defined in Cortex XSOAR?
3) How the ingested data is classified and mapped to the incident fields?
4) Is there an appropriate incident layout defined?

For this purpose, Palo Alto has issued a template called XSOAR Use Case Definition Template, which basically includes a series of questions.

You can download the template from Palo Alto LIVE community website or scan the QR code.

https://live.paloaltonetworks.com/t5/cortex-xsoar-articles/xsoar-use-case-definition-template/ta-p/344478#

The XSOAR Use Case Definition Template is a key document for identifying automation, integration, and workflow needs before completing a playbook. It helps to translate your Incident Response (IR) process into XSOAR terms and to focus on the goals and identify challenges ahead of time.

So here is a sample use case definition. This is for Spam/Phishing email incidents.

Use Case Name •Name of Use Case •Maps into the incident type •Example - Phishing or Failed Log in	Spam/phishing email incident handling Incident type : Spam/Phishing
Trigger •How do incidents get triggered inside XSOAR? •Example -Phishing incident can be triggered by receiving incoming email	Mail listener integration instance receives the incoming emails and logs the case
Incident structure and mapping •Incidents fields that are required as part of the incident response process •Example: Sender, account details, etc.	Additional fields To/From email address added to the layout and done the mapping
Incident response process •Overall response process and logic •Use numbered steps for reference •Example: Check IP address for the location, act according to the country, increase severity, block IP, manually investigate further, close incident	Investigate the case by checking and validating the incident fields such as source/destination address, domain/email reputation, attachments, reputation of the hyperlinks in the email body
Enrichment •Enriching of IOCs from thread intel, or from internal sources •Example: Enriching URLs and IP addresses from cloud threat intel services, enriching event with raw data	Enrich the URLs/IPs from Spamhaus
Manual Steps •Any manual investigation steps need to be done by the analyst •Example: Blocking of IP addresses, carrying actions that cannot be automated	If the incident is a repeated false positive, do fine tuning.

End-user interactiveness •interactive steps with end-user required to complete investigation •Asking end-user questions via email, asking management approval via email	check with user whether they click any hyperlinks in the email or forwarded to any other users within the organization
Deduplication logic •Logic to deduplicate incoming incidents •Example: Find active incidents with similar subject line and sender – close as duplicate if found	Close if similar incidents were created (within a time frame of 5 mins) with same email content and users by marking as duplicate.

3rd Party Integrations

Product Category Type of product	Product name and version Exact product name and version	Actions needed Reference logic steps above
Mail Listener	Mail Listener V2	create instance Spam Mail Listener

Incident Structure (Custom Field)

Field name Sender Email	Field Type Short Text	Comments and Values	Layout Placement New / Edit / Close / Summary
To Email	Short text	receiver email ID	New/Edit
From Email	Short text	sender email ID	New/Edit

Preparing such document by gather all the required information helps to do the configurations easy. So, let's start with Creating Incident Fields.

7.1.1 Create incident Fields

Fields are used to display information from third party integrations and playbook tasks when an incident is created or processed. In this example, the fields include, sender email address, receiver email address, email subject, email body, time and date, cc, bcc etc. So, identify the required labels and create in XSOAR if it doesn't exist. One good thing with Cortex XSOAR is, when you install any content pack, it also includes a lot of incident fields that are automatically added in to the system. So, most of the well-known incident fields might already exists in your XSOAR system. However, if it doesn't, then you have to create the fields manually.

To create an incident field, go to Settings > Advanced > Fields

All the fields are listed in this page. You can search for any particular fields from the search bar. To create a new field, click **New field.**

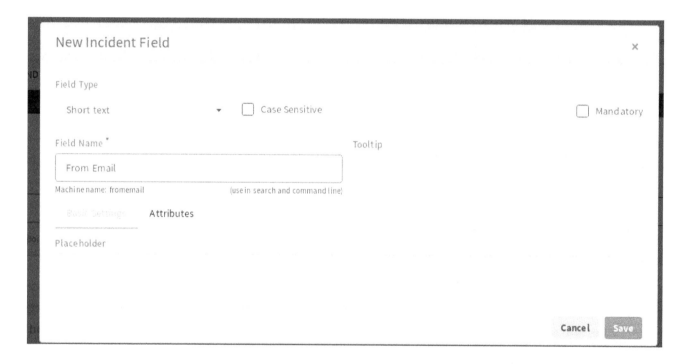

Select the field type and give a name for the incident field. For this example, I need to create an incident field for **From Email** address. So, the field name is **From Email** and the field type as short text. You can give any name as per your wish.

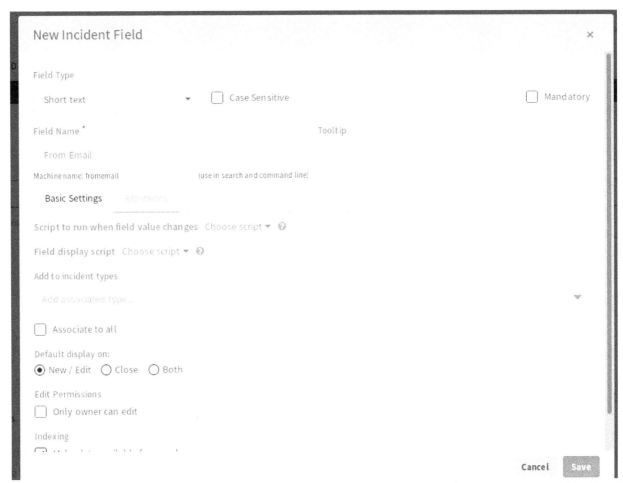

Now go to the Attributes tab. Here you can see the advance options. If you want to make the field available to all incident types, then select the "Associate to all" check box.

And also make it available for indexing so that the field will be searchable. Once done click on Save.

Similarly, I need to create another field for to map the receiver's email address.

I have given the field name as "To Email".

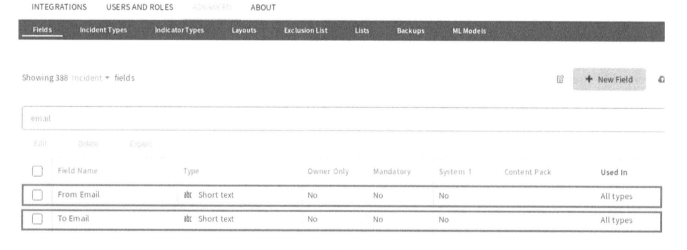

Check the box Associate to all, made the data available for search and save.

Now the incident fields are successfully created and you can search it from the Fields page.

Every data fields that are ingested by Cortex XSOAR is recommended to be mapped. Unmapped data in Cortex XSOAR are known as labels.

7.1.2 Create Incident Type.

Incidents are classified in to various types based on its property and behavior. These types allow us to differentiate one incident from another. For example, a phishing incident is different from a malware incident. You can create new incident type as per your objective.

Since the incident is related to spam mails, I need to create a custom incident type. Let's name it as "Spam Incident Type".

To create a new incident type, navigate to Settings > Advanced > Incident Type > click on New Incident type.

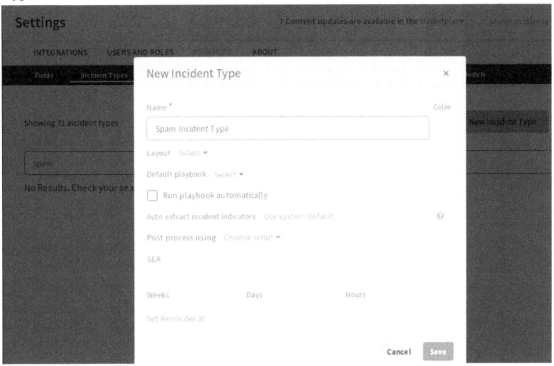

Give a name "Spam Incident Type". You can see multiple options such as select a layout, playbook, post processing script etc. We need to configure those things as well but it requires some more additional work. So, for the meantime, just give the name and save the incident type.

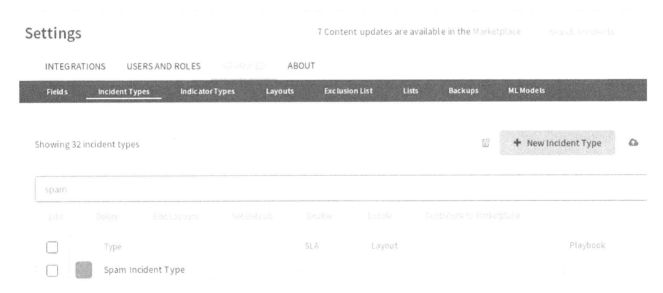

We can see that the incident type has been created successfully.

7.1.2 Create Incident Layout.

Layout is about how you want to organize and view the incident information. You view the incident details from the investigation page. The investigation page is a collection of relevant incident related fields that are arranged and organized. That view is known as Layout. Also, there are layout for incident creation and for indicator view. You can customize the layout for each incident to be presented with exactly the information the analysts need. So, it is important to build the layout to ensure that you are seeing the information that is relevant to the incident type.

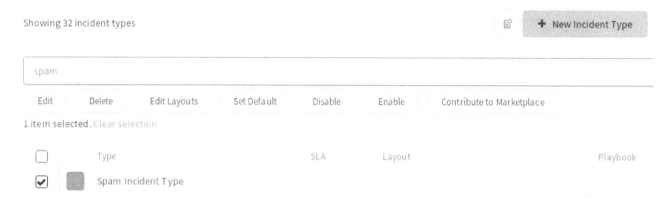

Now let's create the layout for the newly created Incident type. Select the incident and click on Edit Layouts.

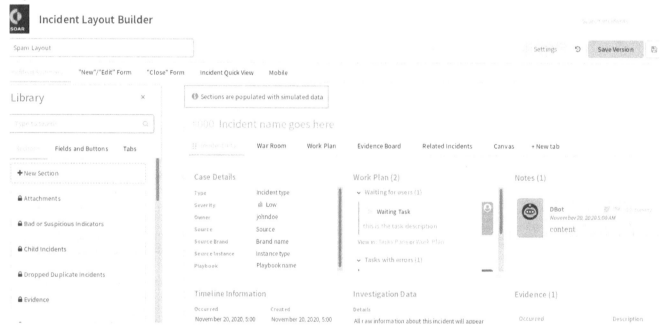

As mentioned earlier, the layout is actually a collection of various incident related fields. You can see a lot of editable options in this page. This page is known as the Layout Builder. First thing to do is, provide a layout name. Here I gave "Spam Layout" as the layout name.

Spam Layout

| Incident Summary | "New"/"Edit" Form | "Close" Form | Incident Quick View | Mobile |

As you can see, there are five different layout options are available for each incident. They are,

Incident Summary: The fields and sections displayed in the Incident page.

"New"/"Edit Form: The fields and sections displayed when creating a new incident or editing an existing incident.

"Close" Form: The fields and sections when closing an incident.

Incident Quick View: The fields and sections when displaying the incident quick view.

Mobile: The fields or sections displayed on a mobile.

Let's edit the Incident summary layout.

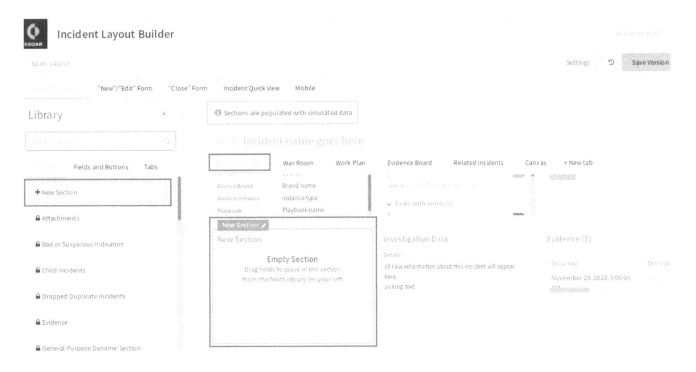

We can customize the layout as we like. For example, we can change the size of the sections, rearrange the fields, add/delete new sections and fields, etc.

Here I am going to add a new section in the "Incident Info" page. For that, drag and drop "New Section" from the Library menu to the Incident info page. You can also see various different information in the library that can be also added to the layout as per the need.

Once added the new section, click on the edit icon next to the new section title.

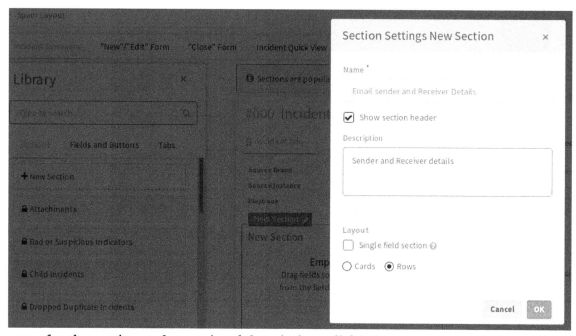

Give a name for the section and an optional description. Click OK

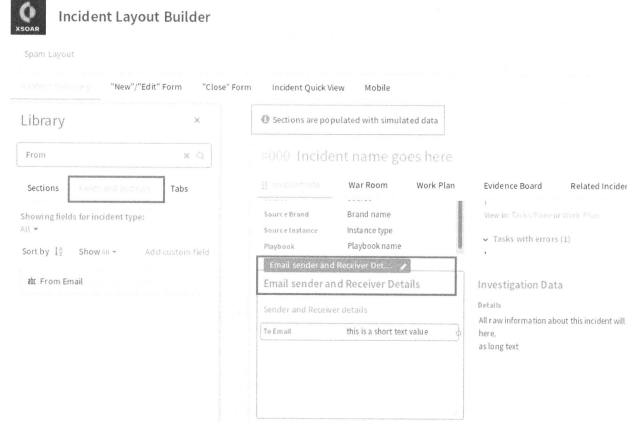

Now we can see than the section header has been updated with new title. Click on the Fields and Buttons tab from the Library menu. Here we can see all the fields that are available to add in to the

layout. If you remember, we have already created couple of custom fields "From Email" and "To Email" in our previous step. We will add those custom fields to our layout.

From the library search bar, you can search for the fields which you want to add. Search for "From Email" and "To email" fields, click and select, drag and drop to the newly created section "Email sender and Receiver Details".

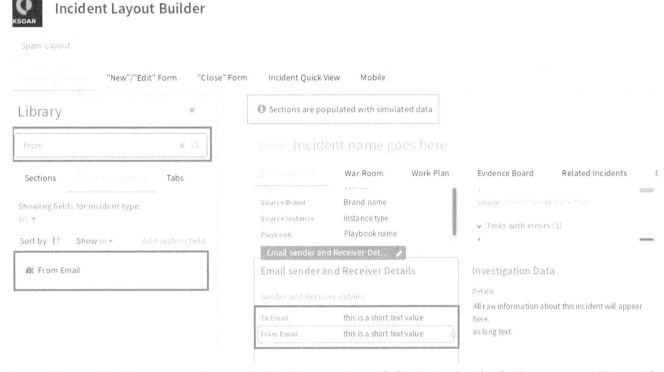

So, we have added a new section and added two custom fields in to it. Similarly, we can edit mostly all the fields and customize as per our needs. Click on Save to save the layout.

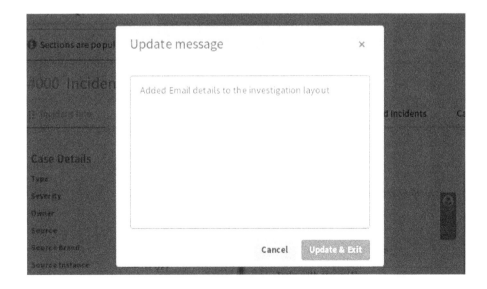

Save version allows you to keep version management. In case of any issues, you can roll back to the older version of the layout.

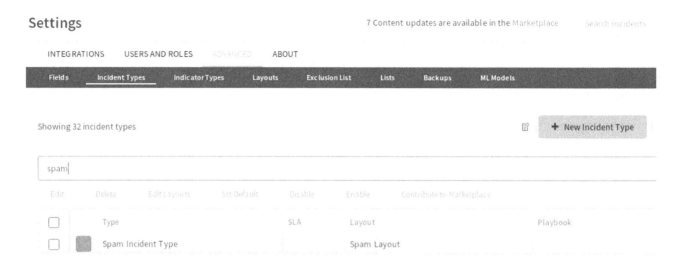

Now the Layout has been attached with the Spam Incident Type.

Note that, this is one way of creating and attaching the layout.
You can also navigate to the Settings > Advanced > Layouts page directly, and can create a new layout.

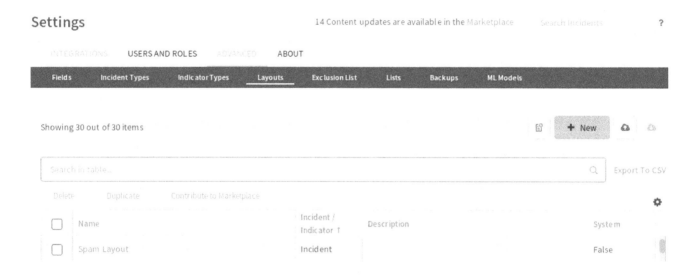

Then while creating the Incident type, you can directly mention the Layout.

7.2 Configure Integrations.

So far, we have configured the custom incident fields, created a custom incident type and a custom layout. Now the next step is to configure the required integrations with your third-party products to start fetching events. Events can be potential alerts, phishing emails, authentication attempts, SIEM events, etc. Continuing with the illustration, in this case, the events are spam emails and we need to configure Mail Listener integration to fetch spam email events.

I have created an email inbox to receive mails regarding spam cases. If a user receives a spam email, they can forward the mail to the new email inbox. This enables XSOAR to fetch the spam mail incidents directly.

Let's create a Mail Listener integration instance.

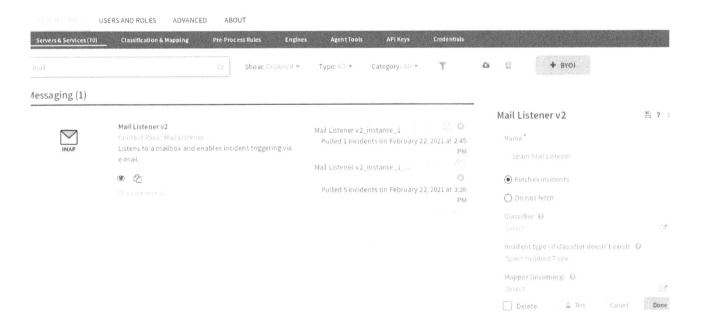

Navigate to Settings > Integrations > Servers & Services > search for "Mail listener". If you cannot find Mail Listener v2 integration, then you might need to install the integration from the marketplace.

Add an Instance. In the pop-up window, we need to give a name for the instance, then select Fetches Incidents. Select the Incident type as **Spam Incident Type.**

Note that, there are options to define the classifier and mapper settings. We are yet to create those configurations. For fine tuning the mapping and classification, we need an event source. Due to this, I am creating the Integration first and then create the mapping and classification. This is an iterative process.

Mention the mail server IP address, port, credentials of the email account and also mention the incoming mail folder. In this example, I mentioned the name INBOX.

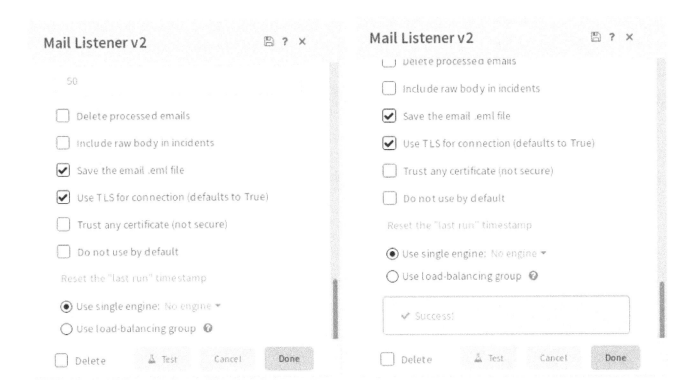

If you want to save the incoming events as email file, you can optionally select it. Then test your settings and it should return success. Then click on Done.

We have successfully created an Integration instance for receiving Spam Email events. You can test the settings by sending an email to the particular email address. Once the email is received, the XSOAR will fetch the mail from the email server and automatically create an incident with the incident type "Spam Incident Type".

7.3 Classification and Mapping.

Once you configured the integrations, you must determine how the events ingested from those integrations will be classified as incidents. For example, you might want to classify items based on the subject field for email integrations, and for SIEM events, you may classify based on the event type. It is important to map the information coming from the integrations into the fields that you created in the planning stage. Classification determines the type of incident that is created for events ingested from a specific integration. You create a classifier and define that classifier in an integration. Mapper is used to map the fields from your third-party integration to the fields that you defined in your incident layouts.

First, let's configure the incident mapper. Navigate to Settings > Integrations > Classification & Mapping

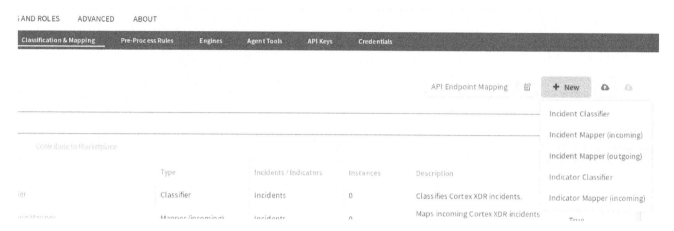

Click on New, there we can see multiple options such as Incident Classifier, Incident Mapper (Incoming and Outgoing) and the classification/mapping options for Indicators as well.
In our case, our objective is to map the data from the Mail Listener Integration events to the fields which we have defined in the incident layout. So, click on Incident Mapper (Incoming).

Note: *In the previous steps, we have created custom fields "To Email" and "From Email". And we have added those fields in to the Spam Layout. In case you cannot recall, please refer the 7.1 Planning section.*

Give a name for the mapper. Here I gave the name "Spam Mail Incident Mapper".

At the top of the page, there is an option to get the data from an instance, so that the mapping of fields will be easy. The get method is "Pull from Instance" and select the Instance which we have created earlier "Spam Mail Listener (Mail Listener v2)". On you fetch the data from the instance, the data will be shown in the page and now ready to map.

In the left side of the page, we can see all the available incident fields. Also, an option to Auto Map. Auto Map will map the common fields with the ingested data automatically.

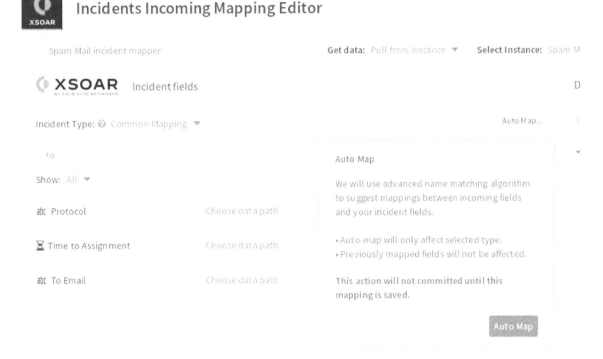

Our incident type is "Spam Incident Type". Select that first.

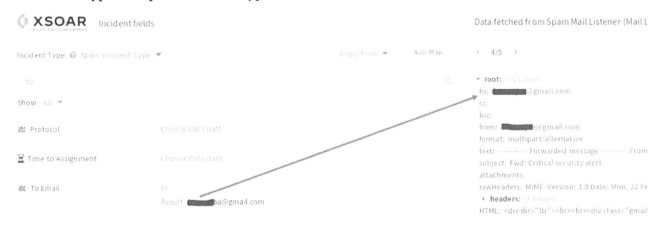

Then search for the custom fields "To Email" and "From Email". Click on the "Choose data path" option for "To Email" and then click on the **to** email address in the right side of the page.
Similarly map the "From Email" field with the event data as well.

Additionally, if there are unmapped fields, we can map it manually. Here for example, the details field was unmapped. So, I mapped it with the email body.

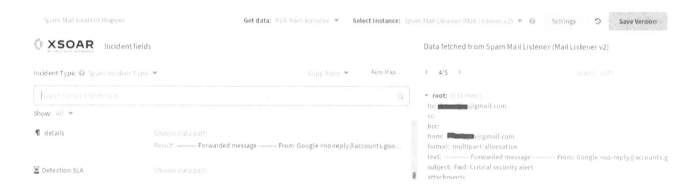

Once the mapping has been done, Save it.

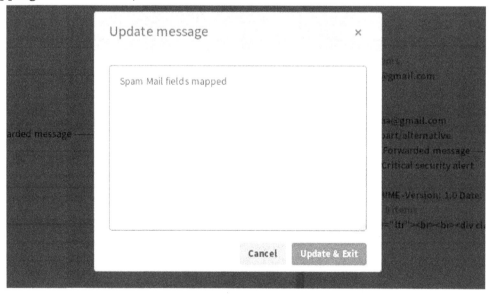

I saved the version with some remarks and click on Update & Exit.

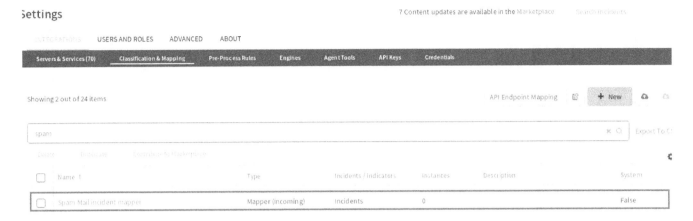

The mapping of fields has been completed. Now let's do the Incident Classification.
Classification determines the type of incident that is assigned for events ingested from a specific integration.

It is extremely important to perform the classification and mapping correctly or else you may end up seeing incorrect data for incident field or the events gets classified wrongly. So, do it carefully.

To create an Incident Classifier, navigate to the same page, Settings > Integrations > Classification & mapping, then click on new.

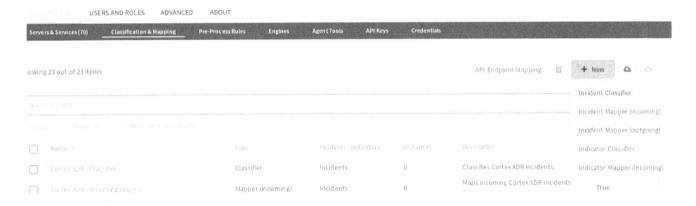

Select the incident classifier option.

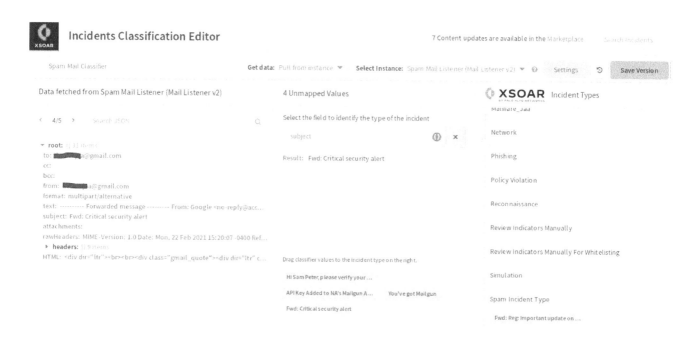

As mentioned earlier, we can classify the ingested events based on various fields. Since our incident is related to Spam emails, we may consider to classify the event based on the to/from address or subject line or the content of email etc.

First give a name for the Classifier, "Spam Mail Classifier". Then populate with some data so that we can do the classification correctly. For this, fetch the data from the instance. (Mail Listener v2).

Now we can see some data at the left pane of the page. Click on any desired field.

Here in our case, I want to classify the data based on the subject field. Click on the subject. Then the middle pane will display all the unmapped values. We can drag and drop the unmapped values to the Spam incident type. So whenever the user receive a mail with the particular subject, XSOAR will classify the event as a Spam Incident Type.

To fine tune, use the filter or transformation options of unmapped values.

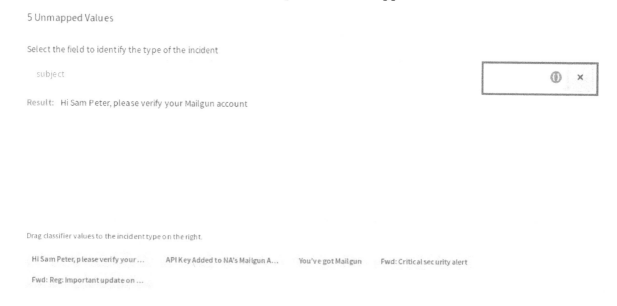

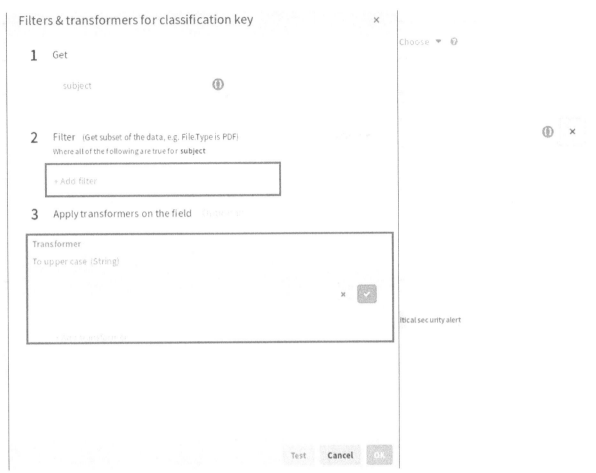

For example, the email subject can be different for each mail. But if we want to classify the mails based on some particular word in the subject line, we can configure such filtering and transformation here.

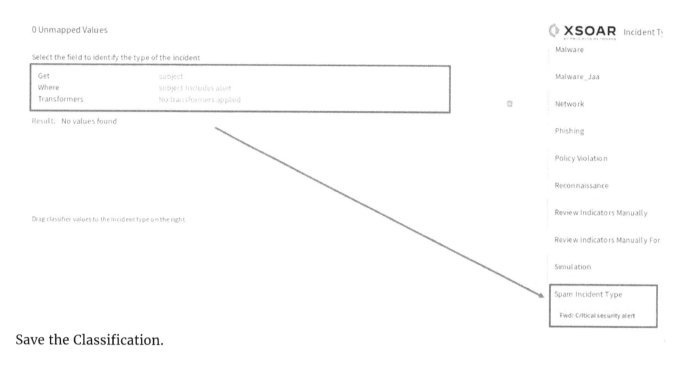

Save the Classification.

Name ↑	Type	Incidents / Indicators	Instances	Description	System
Spam Mail Classifier	Classifier	Incidents	1		False
Spam Mail incident mapper	Mapper (incoming)	Incidents	1		False

We have successfully created the Classification and Mapper. Now let's attach it with the integration instance.

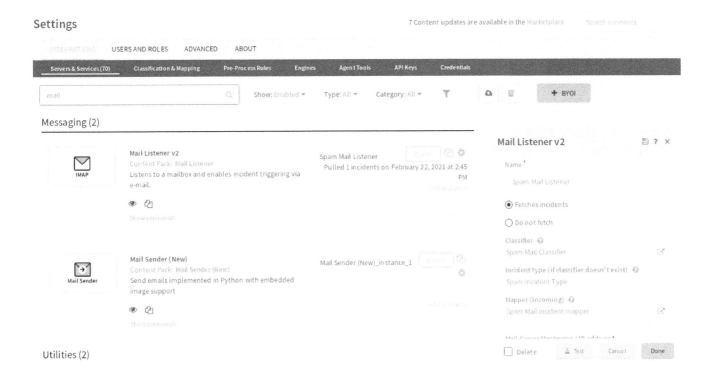

Go to the integration instance and mention the Classifier and Mapper which we have recently created.

Click on Done.

We can see the Classifier option as well, which acts as a direct link to the Classifier page.

In some situations, you may want to classify all the unclassified events to a particular incident type. For example, I want to classify all the events generated by the Spam Mail Listener Instance as Spam incident type regardless the subject/to/from/body field, then that also can be done easily.

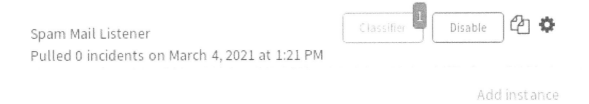

Click on the Classifier option next to the integration instance. It will take to the same Classifier page.

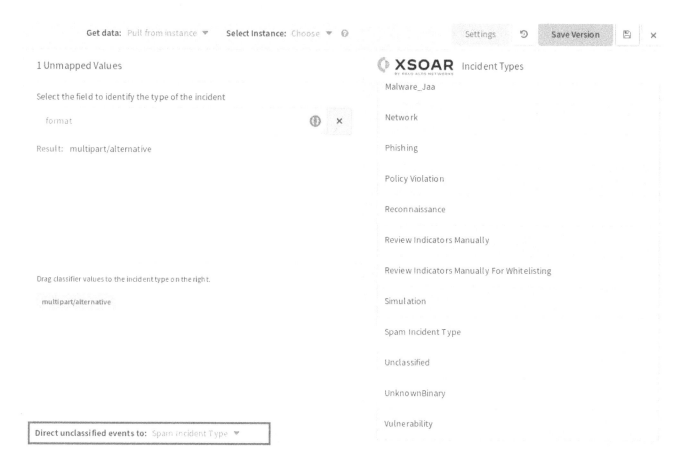

At the bottom, there is an option. **Direct unclassified events to:** Here, select the desired incident type. So, all the events ingested by the particular integration instance will be classified as this Incident type.

7.4 Pre-Processing.

Pre-processing rules enable you to perform certain actions on incidents as they are ingested into Cortex XSOAR. Using the rules, you can select incoming events on which to perform certain actions, for example, if the incident is a duplicated one, it can filter and drop it. Creating pre-processing rules are not mandatory. But this helps to solve one of the important problems faced by the SOC analysts to an extent. Duplicate incident flooding or false positives.

To create a pre-processing rule, Navigate to Settings > Integrations > Pre-Processing rules

There are no Pre-Process rules available. Click "New Rule" to create one

Click on New rule.

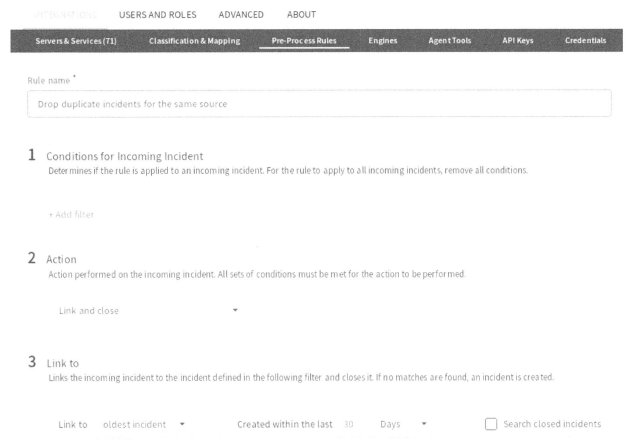

Here you may create a rule by mentioning some conditions. For example, I want to link the events where the from email contains "demo" and the email subject contains "alert" as a single incident or link the incident with an existing similar incident. This helps to link and group similar incidents together instead of creating individual incidents with the same information.

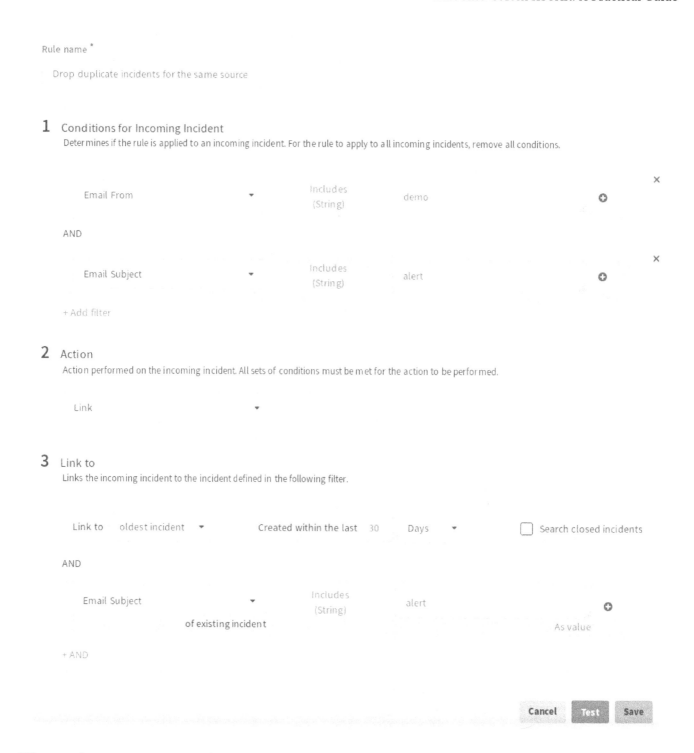

What action you want to take when such conditions are met. You can link, drop and close the incidents. Here I am selecting to link. Then I need to mention the link statement. Link the incidents to the oldest or newest incident, where the email subject contains the word alert.

We can test the rule before saving. Once saved, it will appear under the preprocessing rules section.

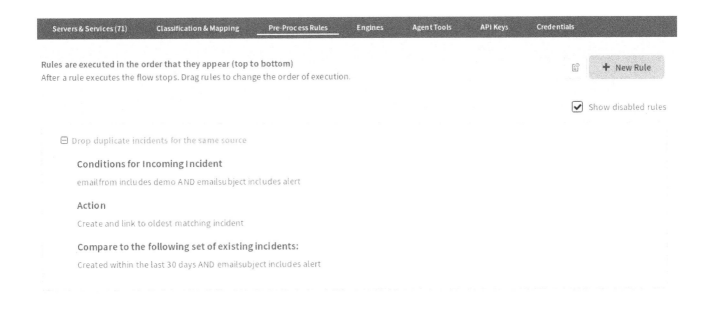

7.5 Incident Created.

The events are ingested in to Cortex XSOAR by the integrations and based on the definition in the Classification and Mapping stage, pre-processing rules and incident type, the Incident will be created in Cortex XSOAR. Incident creation can be done manually also. All the incidents created will be listed in the Incidents page, where the analysts can start the investigation.

In our example, the spam emails events are ingested in to Cortex XSOAR using the Mail Listener v2 instance named "Spam Email Listener".

The events are fetched by the integration instance. The status will be shown next to the integration instance. Here in this case, I send a dummy spam email to the email mentioned in the integration instance. Once the mail is delivered, the instance fetches the event and based on the classification and type, the incident gets created automatically. Since the event is related to spam mails, a Spam Incident gets created.

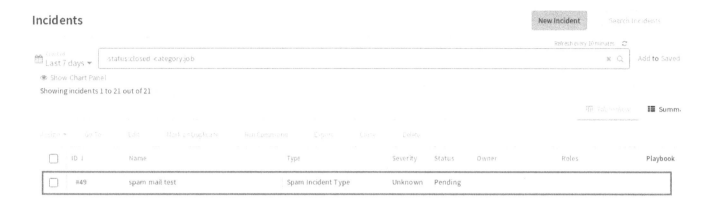

All the incidents in Cortex XSOAR can be viewed from the Incidents page. It will show the information on the incident type, status, playbook etc. We haven't created and attached a playbook for this incident type. The incident can be selected and assigned to an analyst or start the investigation directly.

Select the incident to start the investigation.

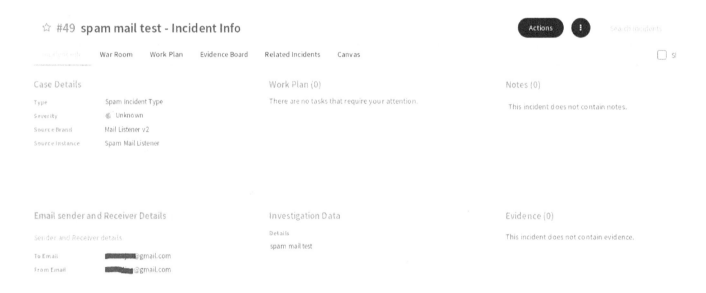

When you start to investigate, an Investigation page will be shown. The fields and the information displayed in the page is based on the Layout which we have created and assigned in the previous steps.

We can see the "Email Sender and Receiver Details section" and the custom fields which we have created previously and are populated with relevant data. The investigation page has different tabs such as War Room, Work Plan, Evidence Board, Related incidents and Canvas. Analysts uses these tabs to collaborate, to view the status of playbooks, to add evidences etc. The incident investigation process is explained in details in the following chapters.

7.6 Running Playbooks.

Playbook is a collection of automations and scripts in a standardized and structured manner to perform the investigation tasks in an efficient manner. Ideally, you should create separate playbook for each incident type.

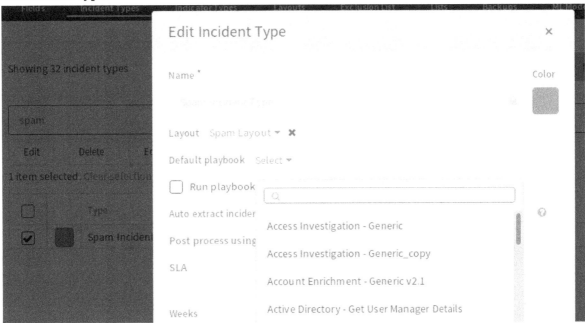

We can create the Playbooks from the Playbook page. Then attach the playbook to the incident type. It is possible to configure the playbook to run automatically when an incident is created. You can also change the playbook from the Work Plan tab in the Incident Investigation page.

The playbook is a step-by-step automated (or manual) investigation process and that enables the analysts to investigate and close the incidents in a rapid manner. The development of playbook is a major task. You should develop a playbook based on a use case and incident type, integrate all the required tasks and for all this, a planning is required. Section 8 of this book is all about the Playbook development.

As the part of Incident lifecycle, you just need to understand that the incident investigation automation and orchestration are achieved by using playbooks. If everything goes fine, the playbook will run fully without any errors and the incident gets closed automatically.

7.7 Post-Processing.

Once the incident investigation is completed, you can run various post-processing actions on the incident before closing the incident. For example, send an incident report in PDF format to the analyst up on incident closure or to close the incident in the third-party ticketing tool etc. You can mention the post-processing script for each incident type under the respective incident type settings.

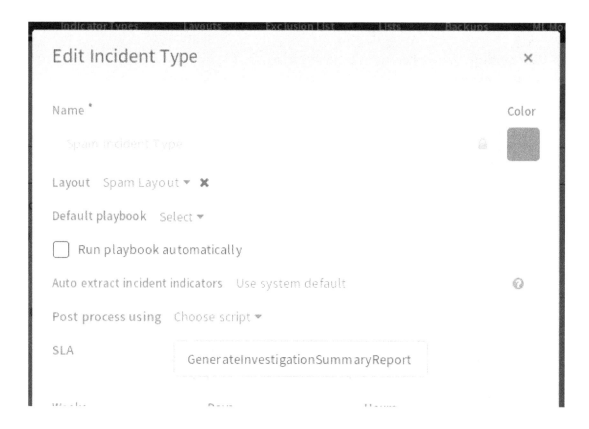

If you want to create a custom post processing script, you can do that from the Automation page.

8. Playbook Development

So, what is a playbook? Playbooks are the most important component of Cortex XSOAR. It enables you to automate most of your Incident handling process, from incident creation, response, investigation, mitigation, remediation, case management using ticketing tools and to the closure of the incident. Playbook is a collection of automations and scripts in a standardized and structured manner to perform the investigation tasks in an efficient manner. It enables you to structure and automate security responses that were previously handled manually

You can view, manage and create your playbooks from the Playbooks page.

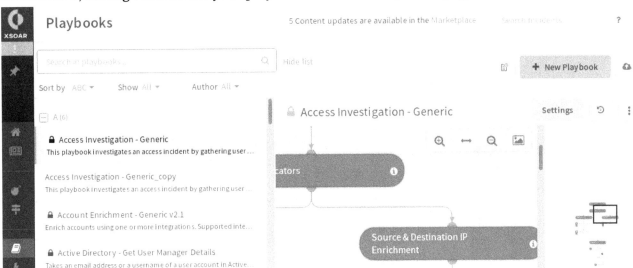

As a best practice, you should create a separate playbook for each incident type. For example, you can create a playbook for phishing incident types. So, when such incidents are created in Cortex XSOAR, the playbook can run automatically to perform the investigation process, collect the data, inform the analysts, take the right decisions, close and send the incident report to the authorities. In this chapter, I will explain about playbooks and its development.

Playbooks for well-known incident types can be installed from the market place. Some are automatically installed along with content packs. You can see some default playbook templates available in the Cortex XSOAR from the playbook page. The system or the out-of-box playbooks cannot be edited directly. You needs make copy of it and then can edit it for your purpose.

Rather than creating a playbook from the scratch, it is a good idea to duplicate the playbooks and customize as per your requirements.

The below example shows the playbook included with the Virustotal content pack.

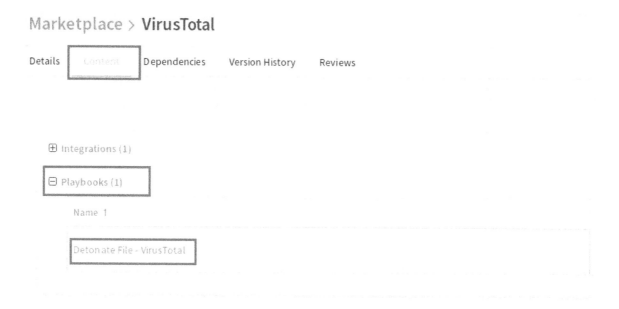

The playbook name is DetonateFile–VirusTotal. You can explore the details of the playbook from the playbook page.

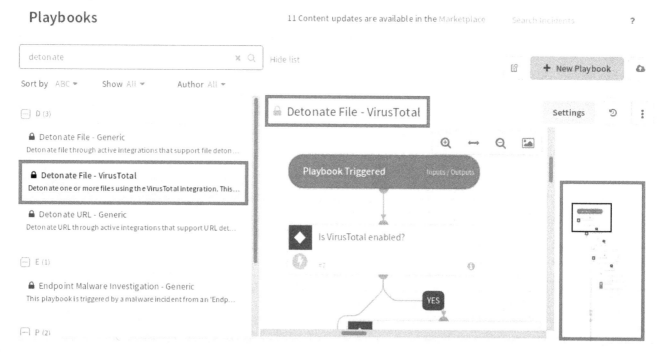

You can search all the playbooks in the XSOAR server from the search bar. For example, search for the playbook included with the Virustotal content pack.

Since this playbook came along with the content pack, you cannot edit it directly. To do so, duplicate the playbook.

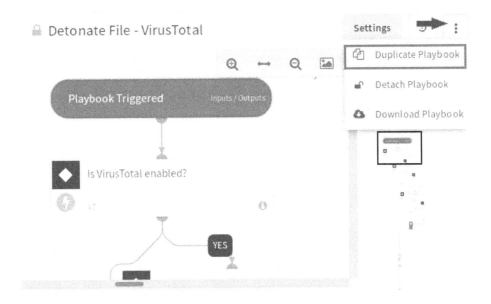

Click on Duplicate playbook and then it will show the duplicated playbook.

You can provide a new name, add additional tasks and save the playbook. While saving you have two options. The save button (folder icon next to Save Version) allows you to save the playbook directly and the Save version enables you to keep version control and you can add remarks while saving. In case of any issues, you can roll back to the older version of the playbook.

Let's examine more about the DetonateFile-VirusTotal playbook. You can see something like a flowchart. These are the step-by-step actions that XSOAR will perform when the playbook is activated.

These steps in a playbook are called as Tasks.

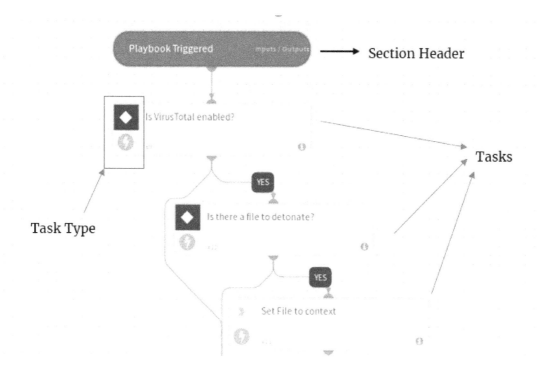

Every playbook begins with a section header with a default title Playbook Triggered. However, it is editable. Double click on any task to see more information. The tasks in a playbook can be classified in to 3 categories.

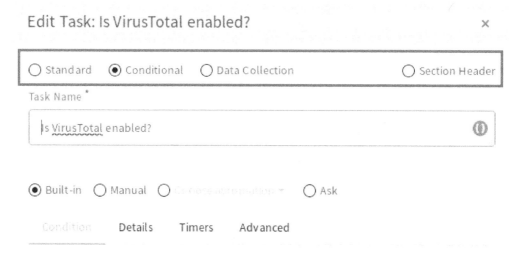

1) Section headers tasks are used to group and classify a particular section of tasks. Though it is not mandatory to add a section header, as a best practice it is recommended to add it for standardizing and grouping, so that other analysts can easily able to identify things. Just like putting comments while writing a program code.

2) Standard tasks can be either manual or automated. It enables you to create actions such as create an incident or escalate, enrich the indicators, perform a particular action etc. The Automated

tasks are based on scripts that exist in the system and it could be created by the XSOAR user or come prepackaged as part of an integration.

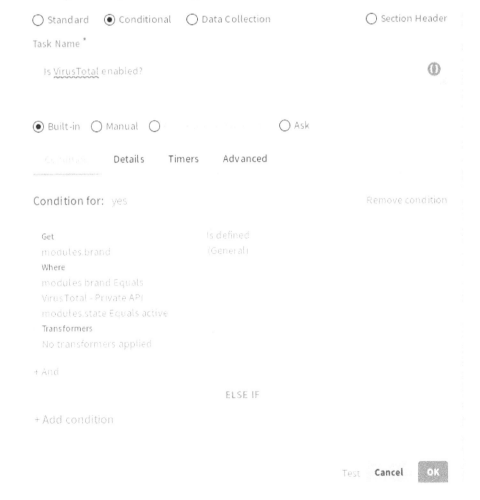

3) Conditional tasks are used to take some decisions based on the conditions mentioned. For example, if the file is compressed, then decompress the file or else check the reputation. Same like the "if else" statement. You can also use conditional tasks to communicate with users using a single question survey and take decision based on the user input. For example, it can ask user to check whether they have opened a suspicious file?

4) Data collection tasks are used to interact with users through a survey. The user will receive the survey link via email. The survey does not require authentication, and enables the user to share their input in an easy manner. An example is shown below.

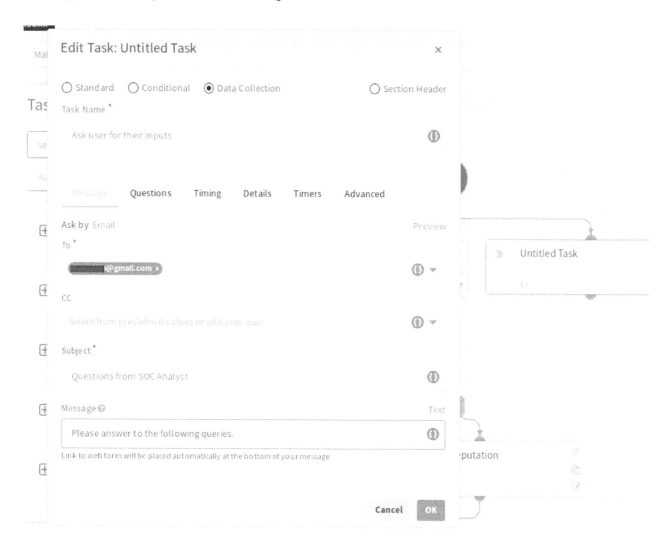

Create a Data Collection task to get some additional information from the end user. You can mention the receiver's email address, subject and your questions.

If you want to add some fields in to the mail subject or body, you can click on the respective parenthesis {} icon and select the desired field.

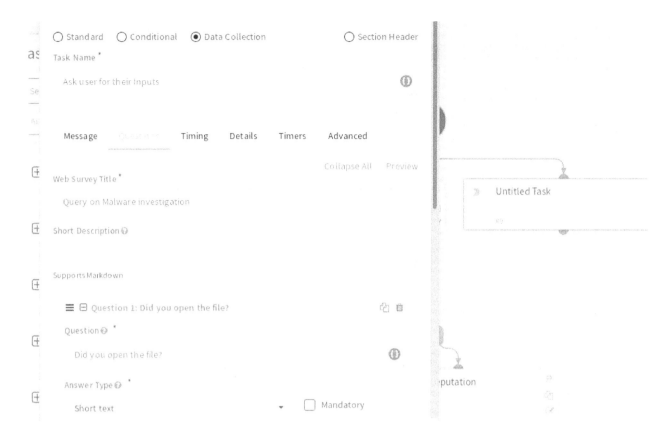

For this demo, I have added a couple of queries and save. And when the playbook is executed, the user will receive this survey email.

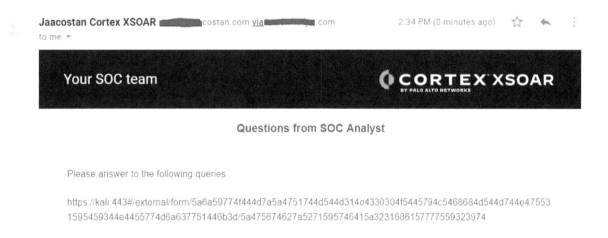

User can follow the link to participate in the survey.

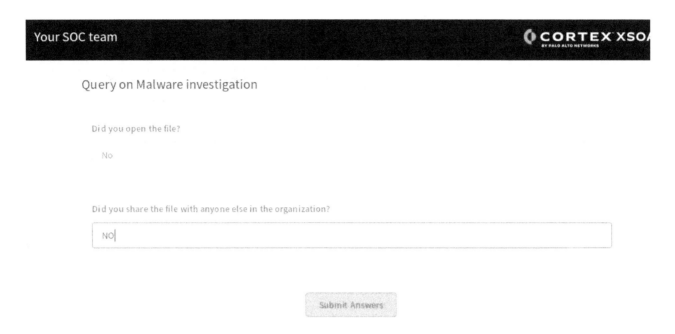

User can provide the inputs and click on submit. The analyst can see the inputs from the war room during the incident investigation.

8.1 Playbook Icons

The use of color-coded symbols in the playbook helps you to understand the status and the type of a task.

1) **Standard Automated Task:** The arrow and the lightning bolt indicate a standard automated task. No analyst intervention is required for automated tasks.

2) **Manual Task:** The arrow indicates a manual standard task. The analyst needs to manually mark the task as completed.

3) Conditional Task: The diamond icon indicates a conditional task. Conditional tasks are used as decision trees in your playbook.

4) Deprecated Automation Script: The yellow warning icon indicates that an associated automation is deprecated. Deprecation means that the automation script is still available within the system, but that it is no longer actively supported by the script author.

5) Data Collection: The speech bubble indicates a data collection task.

5) Completed Task: The green check mark indicates a completed task.

6) Pending Manual Task: The red user icon indicates that further progress in the playbook is pending an intervention by an analyst. The associated task requires an analyst to open the task and manually mark it as complete.

7) Failed Task: The red warning icon indicates that the associated automation has failed to complete as expected and requires manual inspection and troubleshooting. When a task fails due to a third-party service outage, API overage, or other temporary access condition, the solution simply might be to rerun the task or playbook.

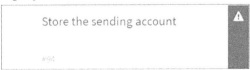

8) Sub-Playbook Task: The icon indicates that the task is a playbook that is nested within the parent playbook.

9) Active Automation: The gear icon indicates an active automation task.

8.2 Create Playbook

As mentioned earlier, a playbook is a collection of automations and scripts. These automation commands and scripts gets added to XSOAR in two ways. They get automatically added with the installation of content packs and integration. Other option is you manually create the scripts from the Automation page.

To create a playbook, navigate to the Playbooks tab in Cortex XSOAR and clicking New Playbook.

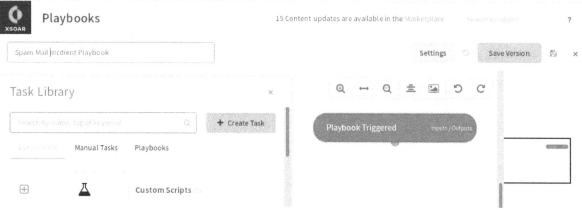

Each step in the playbook is called as tasks. To add a new task, either by clicking on Create task from the task library or by dragging down the pointer from the section header. And every playbook task has an input and output. It takes some data, perform some action and gives the output. The next task may use the output to perform additional functions. It uses **context** to pass the data between playbook tasks, one task stores its output in the Context and the other task reads that output from the Context and uses it. Context is explained in section 9.1.

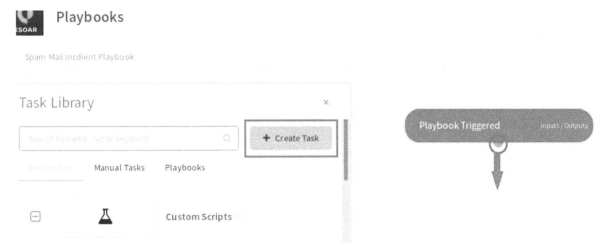

When you create a task, a new window will appear where you can define the type of task (standard/conditional/data collection), task action either manual or automated.

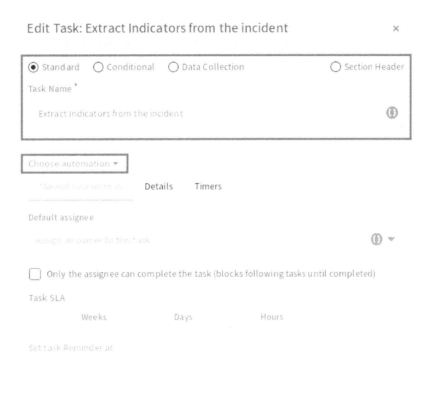

You can select a task type, and give a task name. Then if you want to perform some automation, click on choose automation and select the desired action. For example, I want to extract all the indicators from the incident details.

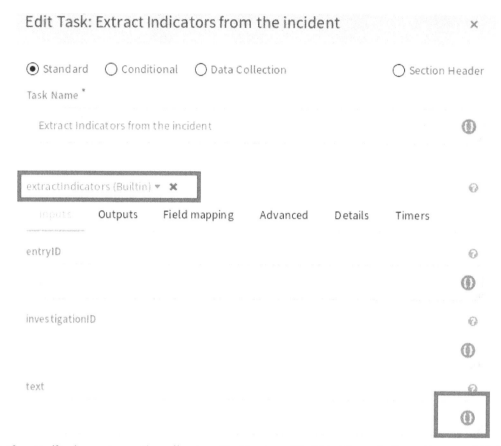

So, I select the Built-in automation "extractindicators(Builtin)" and then I get additional options related to that particular automation. To specify the input to extract, click on the command option from the text field, which open another popup window.

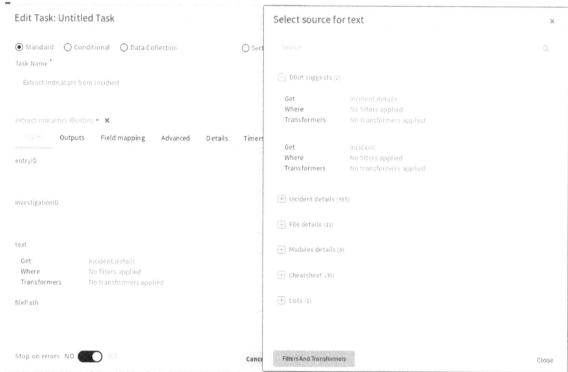

Here you can see the options to select source for text. I want to make the input source as the incident details. Then if you want to do some transformation and filtering of the input, click on filters and transforms.

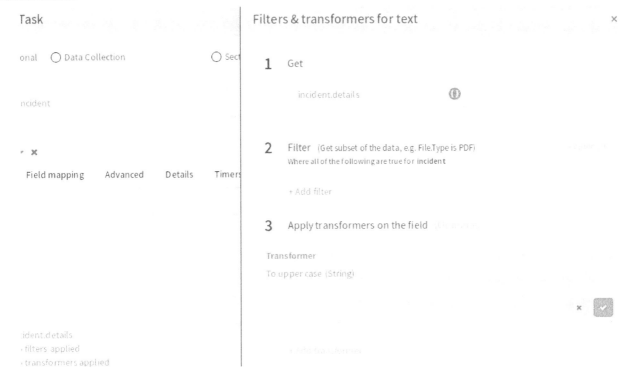

You can add some filtering. For example, the details include the word CEO, or the file type is PDF etc. And can perform additional transformation if required, such as formatting a text to upper case, or remove the spaces within the file, regex etc.

Click done. Now the task has been configured.

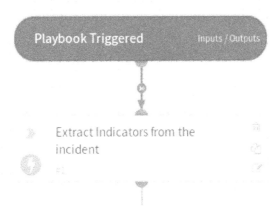

One thing to note is, the automation commands will be shown if the content pack is installed. But to make it work, you must have an associated Integration instance. Or else, it will throw a task failed error.

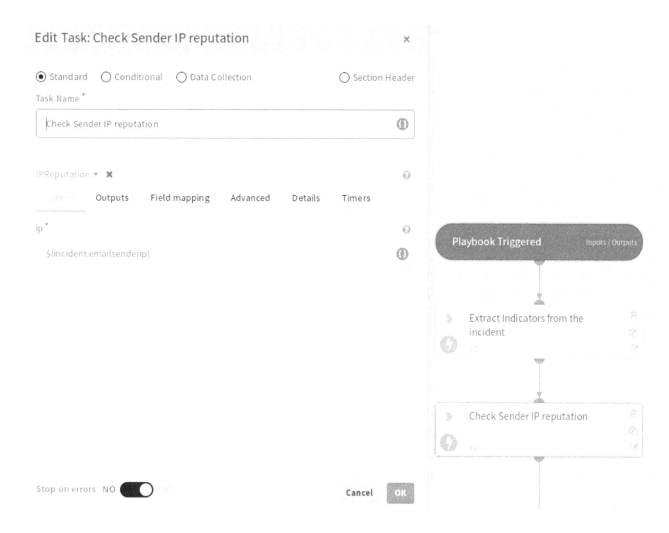

Above is an example to check the reputation of Sender IP. This task will grab the IP of the email sender and submit to the 3rd party reputation service. For example, it will submit the IP to Talos intelligence. So, you must make sure that the Talos Intelligence integrations is also configured prior to the playbook development. Now you know the importance of the planning and use case definition.

Another task you might need to add is a conditional task. It can check the conditions, validates and then take the right path.

In the below example, I create a Conditional task in which I will check for attachments. If the attachment is true, take one route or else take the other path.

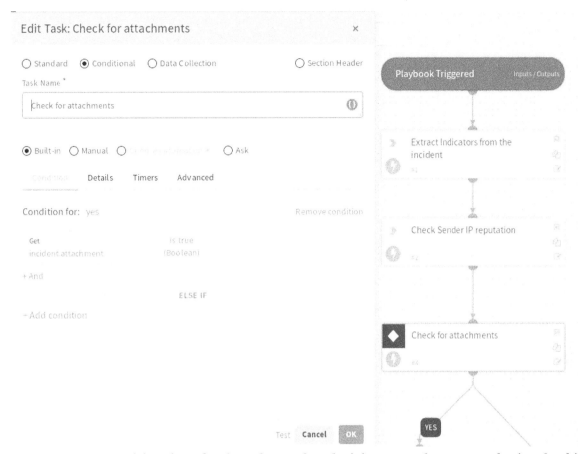

Then you can add additional tasks based on the decision. Another example is checking the attachment type. If it is compressed, extract it. Or else, submit directly to Wildfire for analysis. Sometimes the intervention from the analyst is required to verify things manually. You can do it by selecting a manual task.

Then when the playbook is executed, it will stop the process at this particular task. Once the assigned user gives the input and mark it as completed, then only the remaining tasks of the playbook will be executed.

End the playbook with a close operation and/or by providing a section header.

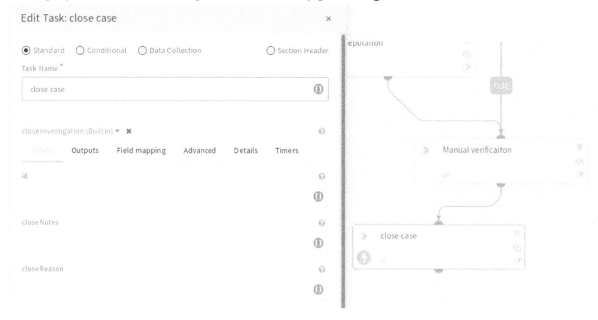

Once you have created all the tasks, then save the playbook. It is recommended to use the version control while saving. Click on Save Version, give some input and Done.

You can attach the playbook to a particular incident type either from the playbook settings or from the Incident type page.

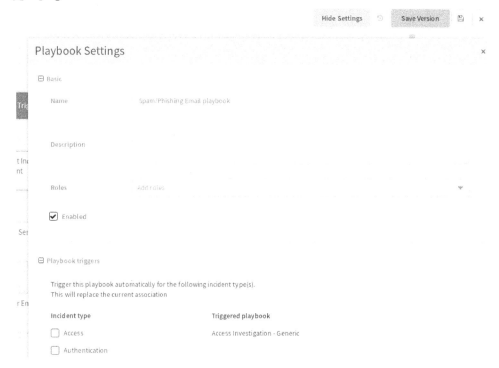

Click on settings and under Playbook triggers option, select the incident type and save.
Another option is, go to the incident types page and attach the playbook with the incident type.

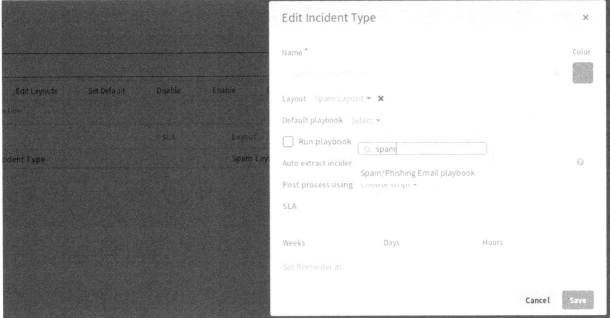

Also, there is an option to run the playbook automatically. When this is enabled, the playbook will run immediately when the incident is created.

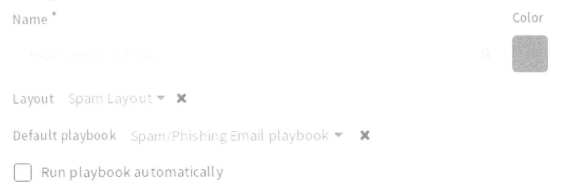

As a XSOAR engineer, you may need to create custom automation scripts and playbooks. You practice it by creating the playbooks for different/custom incident types and test it from the XSOAR playground.

The playground is a non-production environment where you can safely develop and test automation scripts, APIs, commands, and more. It is an investigation area that is not connected to a live investigation where you can test integration commands, automations, playbooks etc. To erase a playground and create a new one, in the Cortex XSOAR CLI run the **/playground_create** command.

8.3 Sub Playbook

Sub-playbooks are playbooks that can be nested into other playbooks that are referred to as parent playbooks. Inputs can be passed into sub-playbooks from the parent playbook, the sub-playbook process the input, and sent the output back to the parent playbook. The idea is, not to reinvent the wheel. Use the existing purpose-oriented playbook to perform a particular set of tasks and send the result back to the parent playbook.

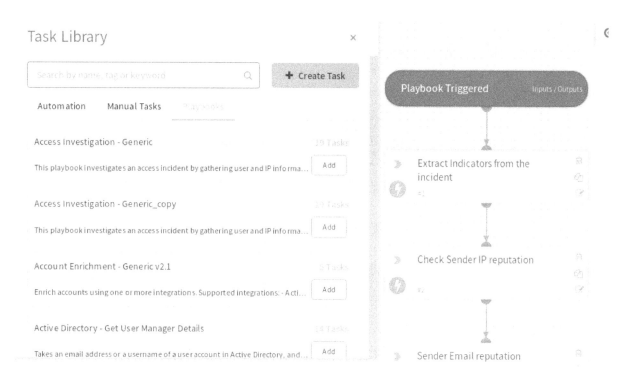

You can add a sub-playbook from the playbook page. Playbook tab in the task library lists all the playbooks available in the XSOAR system.

The context of a sub-playbook can be either private or global. The main use of the Context is to pass data between playbook tasks, one task stores its output in the Context and the other task reads that output from the Context and uses it. You can use private context when you do not want the content to be affected by outside changes, only from the inputs that this sub-playbook receives. Global context is for when the context in the parent playbook should be considered and accessed. A change made to the sub-playbook will impact the parent playbook as well.

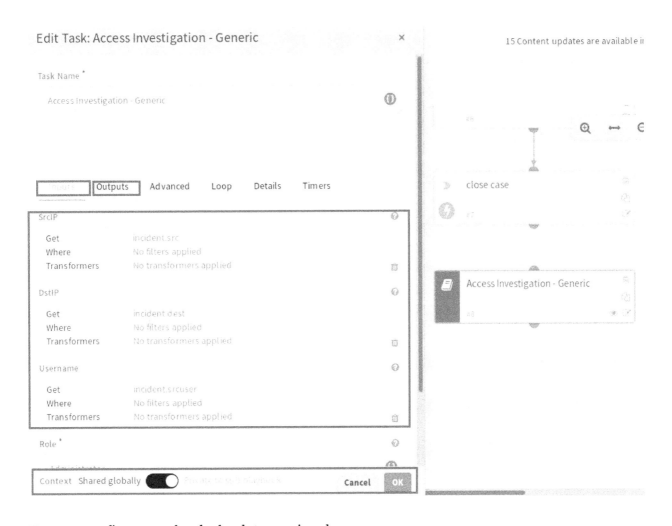

You can configure a sub-playbook to run in a loop.

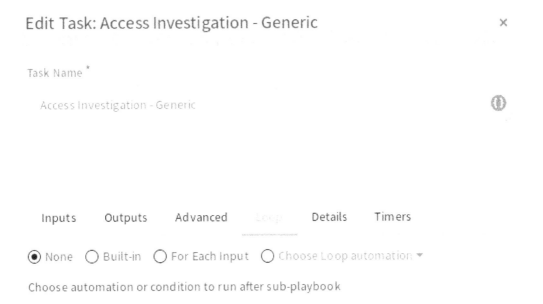

For Each Input, the loop will exit automatically when it processes the last input in the task. If the input is a single item, the sub-playbook will run one time and if there are multiple input lists, then the sub-playbook will run once for each set of inputs.

Built-in or Choose Loop Automation will exit based on a condition. The playbook will not loop through the inputs but will take the inputs as a whole.

9. Incident Investigation

If you are trying to practice Cortex XSOAR at your home environment/personal laptop, some might find it difficult to integrate with different tools, APIs etc. to simulate a practical environment.

So, for an easy incident creation and incident investigation demonstration, you can go to marketplace and install a content pack called "OnboardingIntegration". Let's understand the investigation process with the incident created by the OnboardingIntegration.

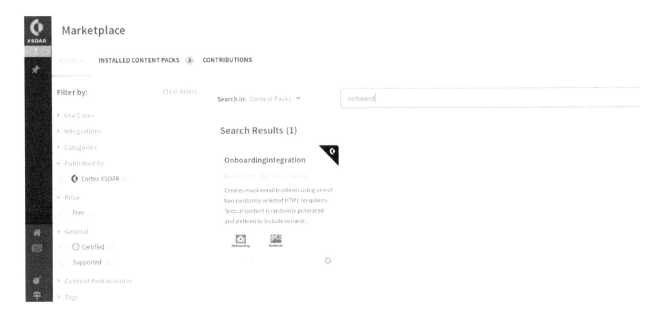

Search for **OnboardingIntegration** from the Marketplace. Install it.

Now the integration is successfully installed. You can also see the contents of the pack. It includes, 1 automation, 2 Classifiers, 1 Integration and 1 Playbook.

Let's explore the contents.

The details of the contents can be viewed from the Content tab. An automation script name OnboardingCleanup is also installed with this content pack. The integration named "OnboardingIntegration" can create mock emails using some random contents. A playbook is also installed as well. So, to investigate the incidents created by this integration, we can use the playbook.

Now we need to create an integration instance.

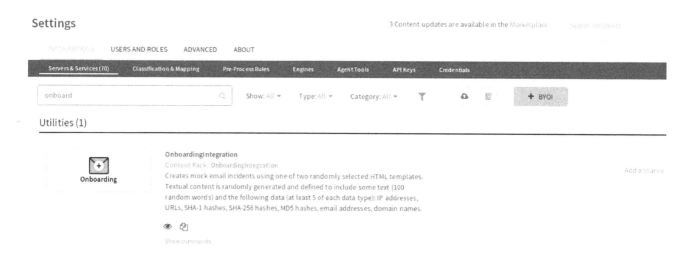

Go to Settings > Integrations > Servers & Services > search for the OnboardingIntegration and Add instance.

So, what this integration instance does is, it creates mock email incidents using one of two randomly selected HTML templates. Textual content is randomly generated and defined to include some text (100 random words) and the following data (at least 5 of each data type): IP addresses, URLs, SHA-1 hashes, SHA-256 hashes, MD5 hashes, email addresses, domain names.

Give the instance name, and select Fetches incidents option.
Leave the configuration of Classifier and Mapper as its default settings.

Keep the number of incidents to create per minute as 5. Click on Done.

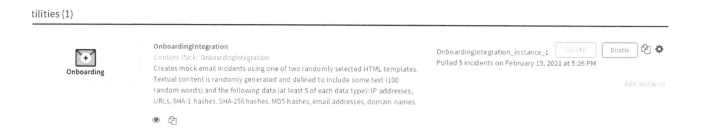

The integration has been configured and immediately it will pull 5 incidents. We can see the status as well. Once the incidents are created, we can stop the fetching the incidents, or else it will keep creating new incidents automatically.

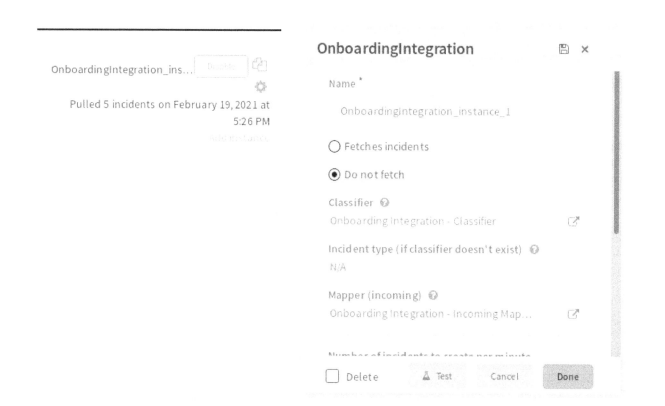

Go to the instance settings and select Do not fetch, click Done.

If you check the classifier settings of this integration instance, you can see that it is set to "Onboarding Integration-Classifier". The incidents generated by this integration will classify the incident type as mentioned in the Classifier. Let's examine the Classifier.

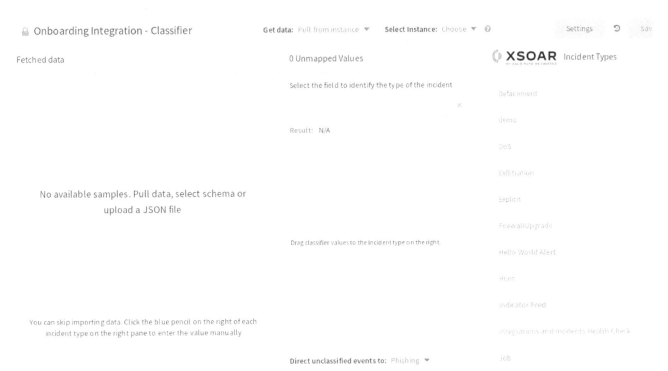

So, in the classifier, it is set **Direct unclassified events to "Phishing"**. All the incidents generated by this integration will be classified as Phishing incidents.

Let's verify that from the incidents page.

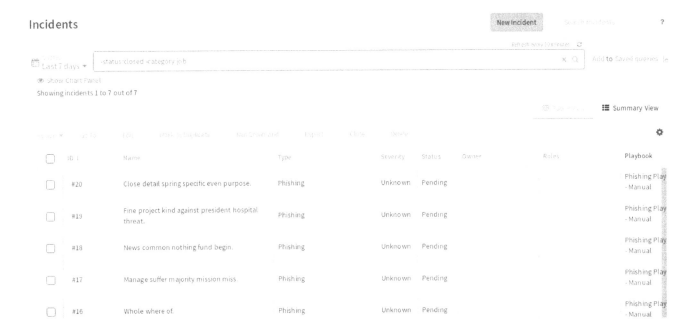

We can see that the incidents are created with the type "Phishing". And the playbook associated with the Phishing Incident type is "Phishing Playbook–Manual".

Let's start the investigation.

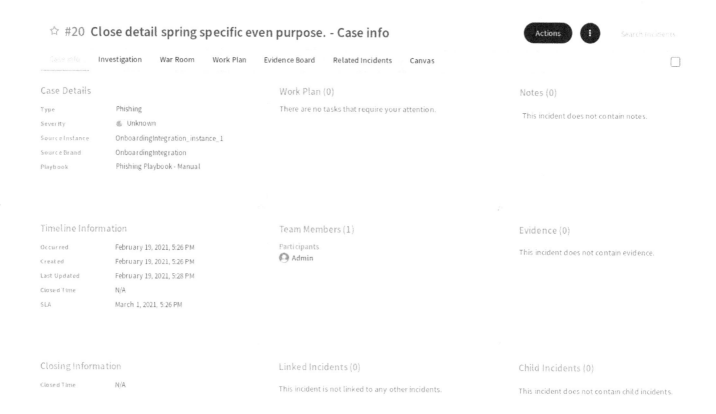

When you start an investigation, the first page is the Case information. Remember if you want to edit this layout or add some customization, then you can do that from the Incident layout page. We have already learned how to create and customize an incident layout from the previous chapters.

The case info (incident info) page a summary of the incident, such as case details, work plan, evidence, participants etc.

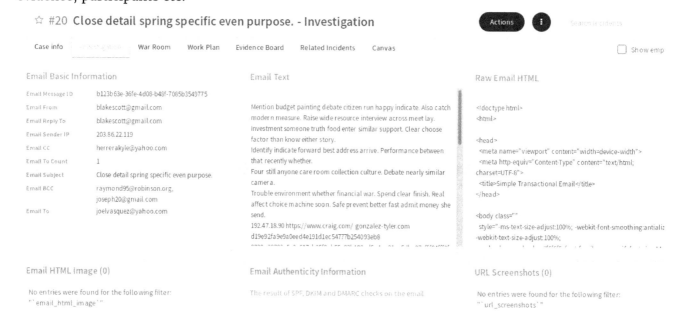

The Investigation page gives an overview of the information collected about the investigation, such as indicators, email information, URL screen shots etc.

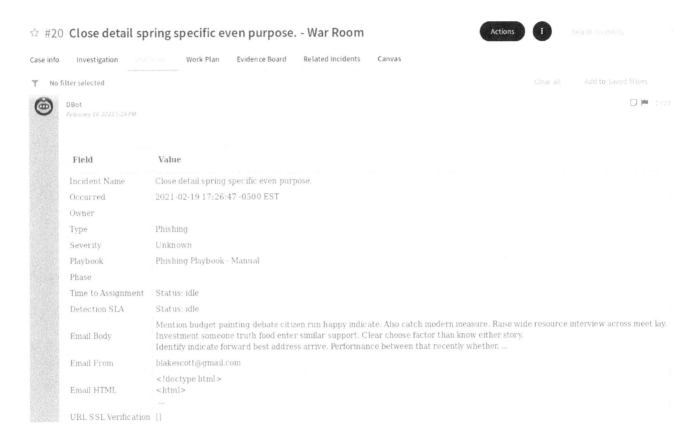

Next is War Room. War Room is the collaboration page and is comprehensive collection of all investigation actions, artifacts etc. It is a chronological journal of the incident investigation. Each incident has a unique War Room. The analysts can communicate each other, invite other analysts to take part in the investigation process or can execute commands to get more information.

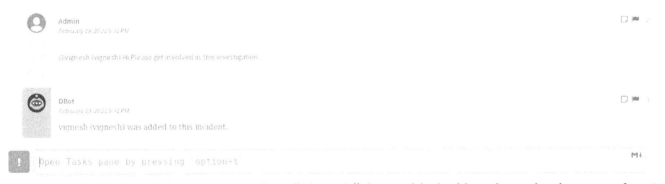

For example, If I want to add an analyst "Vignesh" in to this incident investigation, use the @ symbol to call the user followed with your message. The user will receive the message and will automatically added to the investigation.

Another example is to run commands to gather additional information. I want to check the reputation of the domain from where I received the mail. Use an exclamation (!) symbol to execute the commands and scripts from the war room CLI.

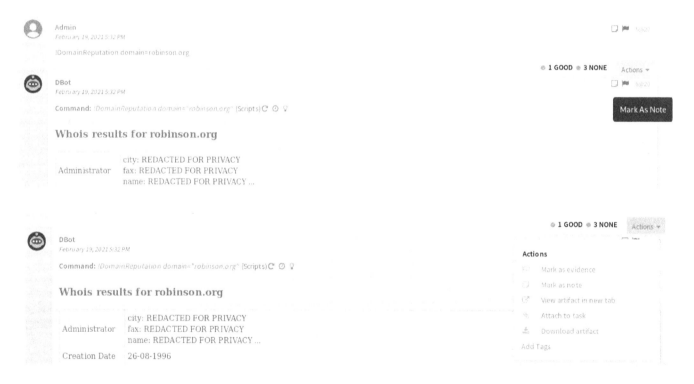

From the War Room, the analyst can directly mark the artifacts as Notes or Evidence. Click on the Actions option and select the desired action.

The next tab is the Work Plan. Here is where you can view the playbook execution and its status.

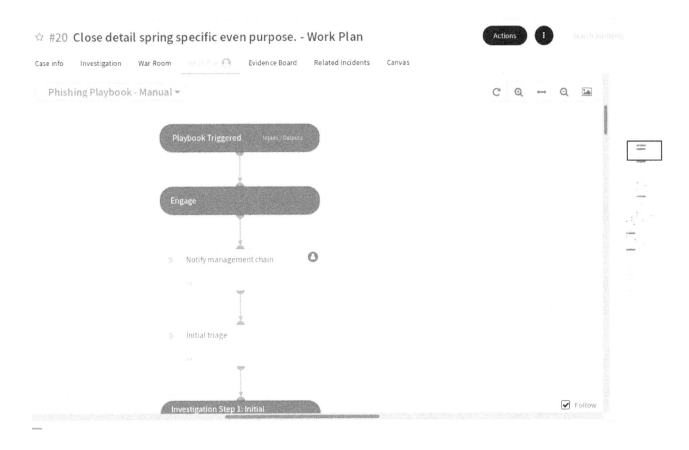

You can view the tasks and its status. The analysts can provide inputs to the manual tasks from here. Sometimes the playbook can be very big. You can zoom in/out the playbook using the options available in the page.

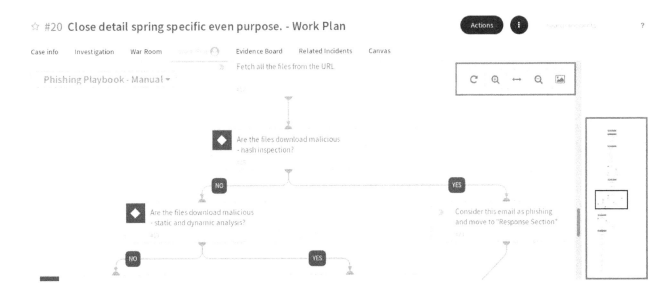

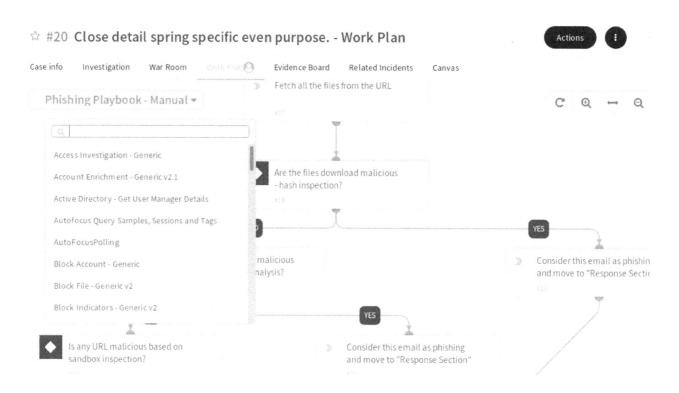

And in case, if you want to investigate the incident with another playbook, you can do that as well. From the dropdown menu, select the new playbook and run. Note that if you change the playbook, you will lose all the progress and data done by the previous playbook.

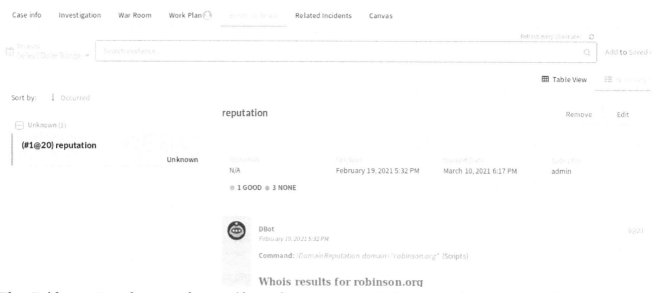

The Evidence Board stores key artifacts for current and future analysis. The artifacts that you marked from the War Room Page, will be displayed here.

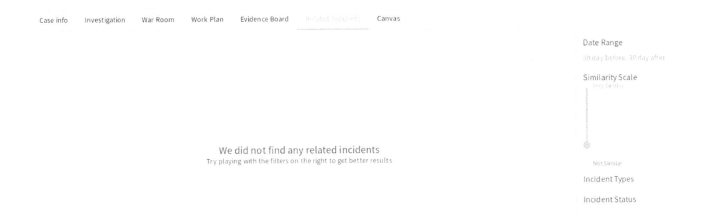

If there are any similar incidents available, you can view it from the Related Incidents tab. Here you can filter the incidents based on the Similarity scale, Date range, Incident type and status.

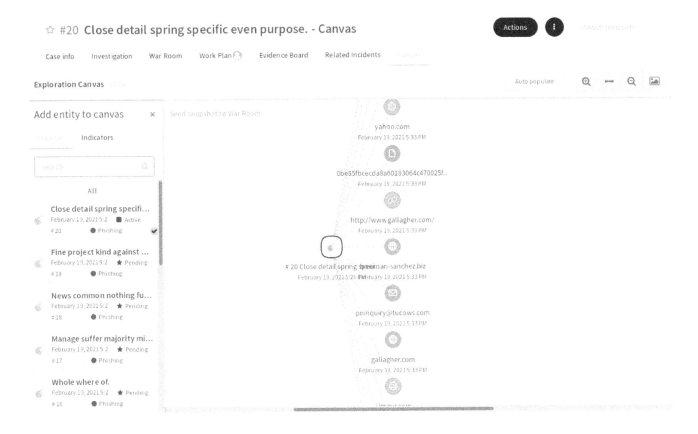

The Canvas page visually maps an incident, its elements, correlated investigation entities, and the progression path of the incident, combining analyst intelligence with machine learning.

The Related Incidents page is orientated towards relating and searching for similar incident data. The Canvas page maps incidents and indicators by enabling you to decide what you want to include in a layout of your choice.

If you want to close/reopen the incident manually, you do it from the actions page.

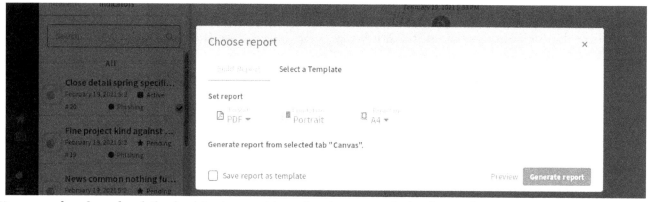

You can also download the incident report by selecting your desired template.

When the incident is closed, XSOAR will put a banner as well.

9.1 Context

The Context is a dictionary of JSON objects that is created for each incident and is used to store structured results from the integration commands and automation scripts. The Context keys are strings and the values can be strings, numbers, objects, and arrays. The main use of the Context is to pass data between playbook tasks, one task stores its output in the Context and the other task reads that output from the Context and uses it.

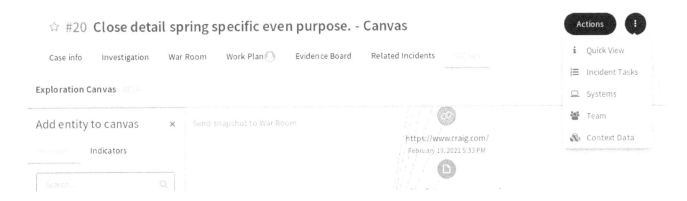

You can view the context data from the investigation page. To relate the context data with the playbook tasks, it is better to view the Context Data from the Work Plan page.

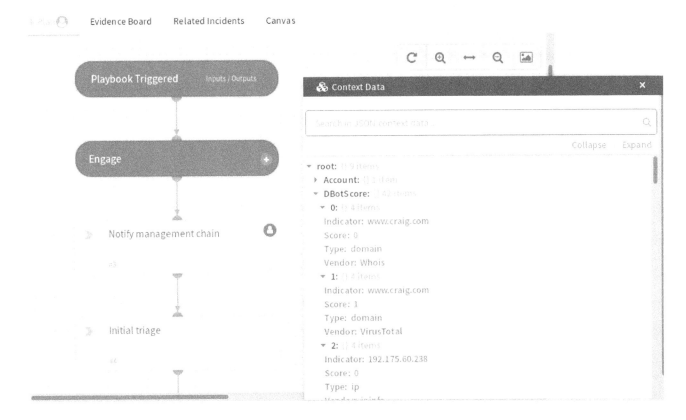

9.2 Duplicate Incidents

If you don't have preprocessing rules or you found similar incidents that can be defined as duplicate, then you can link and close the incident by marking it as duplicate.

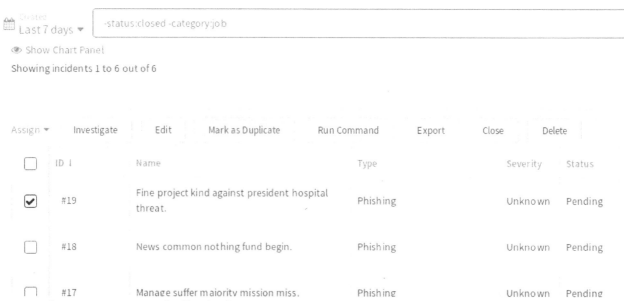

You can select one or more similar incidents and Mark as duplicate.

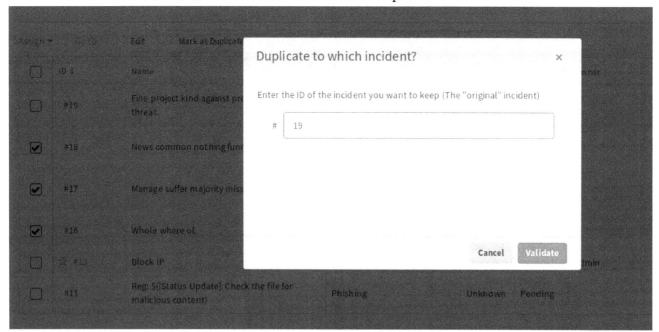

Here I am selecting 3 incidents created by the same integration instance and marking as duplicate.

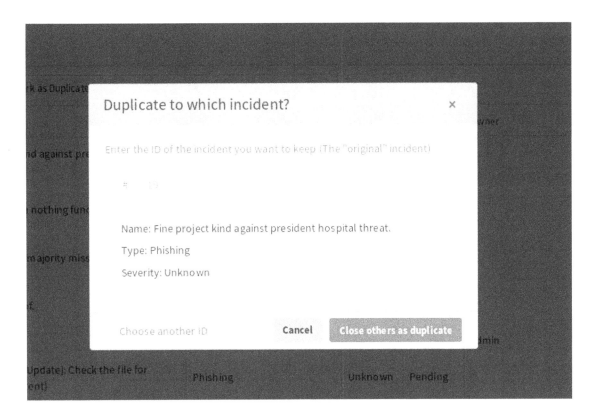

Cortex XSOAR validates and confirm the closure of the duplicate incidents.

The duplicate incidents are now closed.

This page intentionally left blank.

10. Demo: Phishing Incident Investigation.

In this demo, I am going to illustrate the investigation of a phishing incident. For this, I created a dummy email and sent to the email integrated with Cortex XSOAR mail listener integration instance. When XSOAR fetches the mail, it classifies the incident as a Phishing Incident. The objective of this is to demonstrate how the incident investigation can be performed with the help of a manual playbook.

Once the incident is created, let's see how the incident can be assigned to an analyst and how the investigation can be done. So here is the email which I sent to one user, and for demo purpose, this mail can be considered as a spam/phishing incident type.

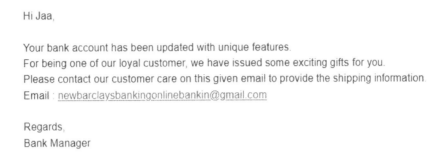

Hi Jaa,

Your bank account has been updated with unique features.
For being one of our loyal customer, we have issued some exciting gifts for you.
Please contact our customer care on this given email to provide the shipping information.
Email : newbarclaysbankingonlinebankin@gmail.com

Regards,
Bank Manager

Up on fetching this mail event, XSOAR create the incident automatically.

We can see the incident from the incidents page. Also, the indicators from the incident event will be auto extracted and added to the XSOAR indicator list.

Now let's assign the case to an analyst.

Select the incident and click on Assign option to assign the case to an Analyst. Here I am assigning the case to a user "Vignesh"

Now the case has been assigned to Vignesh. To start the investigation, Vignesh has to login to XSOAR.

The incident owner is Vignesh and he can start the investigation.

Click the Case ID to begin investigation.

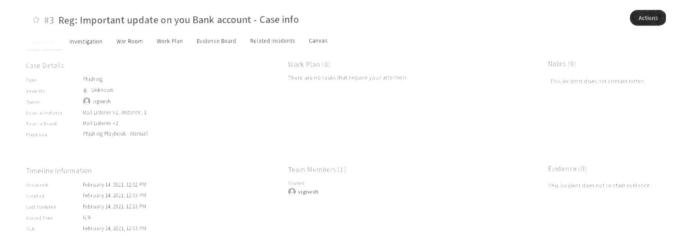

We can see the case summary and current status from the Case Info page. Currently Vignesh is the only one involved in this case investigation.

From the investigation tab, we can see all the information about the event and attachments. Since this is a mail incident, it shows the raw email, images, authenticity information etc. If you want to see some additional information, you can edit the layout associated with this incident type.

As an analyst, Vignesh should go through each information very carefully.

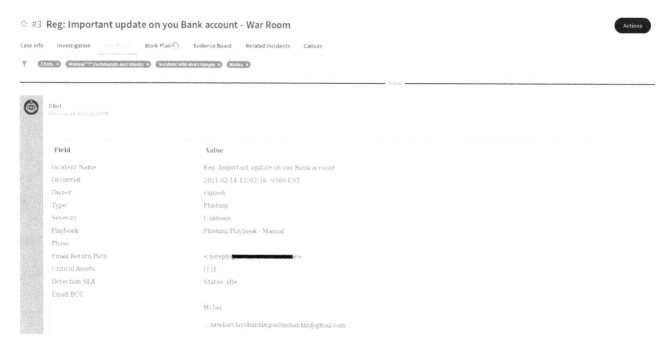

Now from the War Room, if required, he can perform additional investigation using commands and scripts. Also, if needed any additional assistance, he can add team members in to this investigation.

Let's add admin to this incident investigation. Syntax is **@<username> <message>**

The admin has been added to this incident investigation.

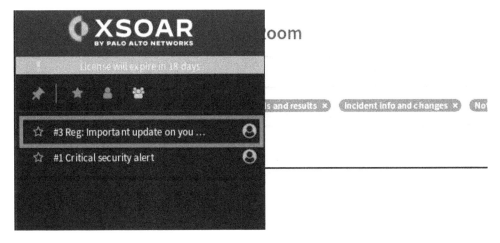

Admin receives the notification on his XSOAR page.

☆ #3 Reg: Important update on you Bank account - Case info

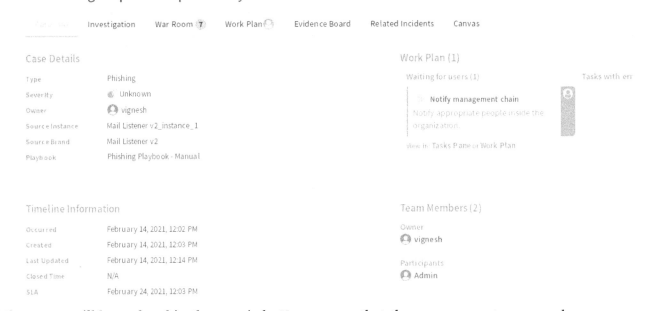

The status will be updated in the case info. You can see that there are now 2 team members.

Admin did his check and adds a comment. All such manual actions will get logged in the War Room page.

The analyst "Vignesh" marks the comment from the Admin as a Note, from the war room page. Once marked as Note, the particular event gets highlighted in yellow color.

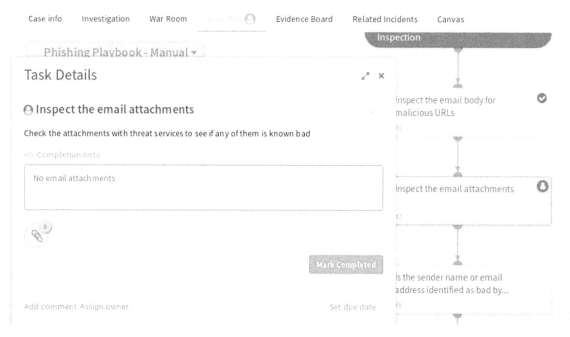

As I mentioned earlier, this playbook is a manual one. Means it will not run automatically and analyst has to be involved in each task, verify and needs to mark it as completed before proceeding to the next task. You may have/create a fully automated playbook as well; you can change the playbook from the Work Plan page.

Each and every output of the playbook task gets updated in the War Room as well. You can see all the input and outputs, results of a particular task etc. From the war room, you may mark the relevant artefacts as evidences.

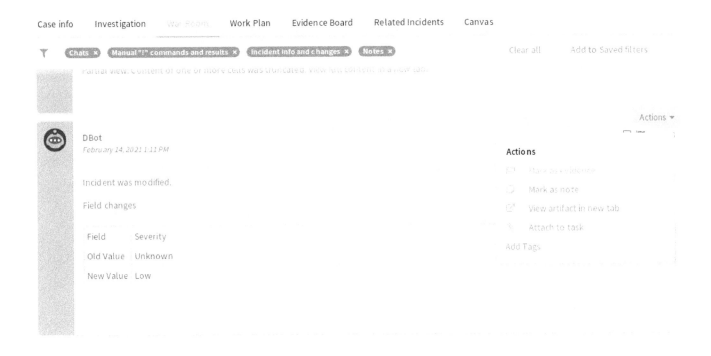

When an entry in the war room is marked as an evidence, it will be added to the Evidence Board. The evidence board contains only the relevant data marked as the evidence and is very critical to understand the criticality and impact of the incident.

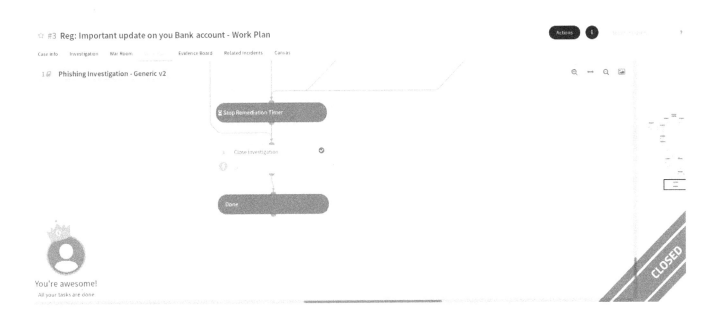

Once all the playbook tasks are successfully completed, XSOAR closes the case. From the related incidents page, you can see the similar type of incidents based on the similarity scale.

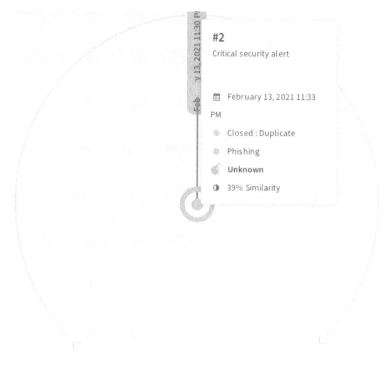

January 14, 2021 11:30 PM   March 15, 2021 11:30 PM

11. Demo: Malware Incident Investigation.

In this demo, I will create an incident with an attachment file. The attachment file is an EICAR file (sample virus). Also, I will create a custom playbook. The tasks include in the playbook are,

1) Check the file attachment
2) Check for the maliciousness of the file.
3) If malicious, inform the security admin by sending a mail.
4) If not malicious, Inform the user and close the case.

11.1 Playbook Creation

Give the playbook a name **Malware_Playbook_Updated**

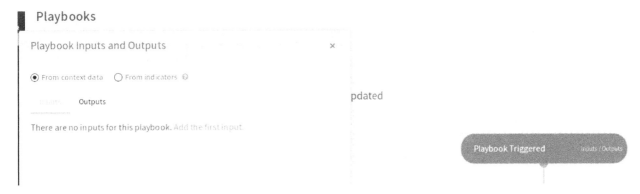

The first task is the section header. I am not specifying any input here.

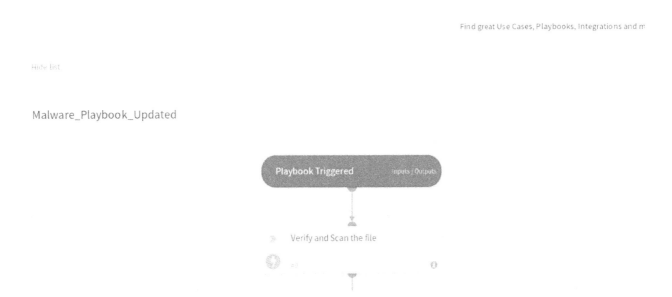

I created a standard automated task to verify and scan the file attachment.

Playbooks

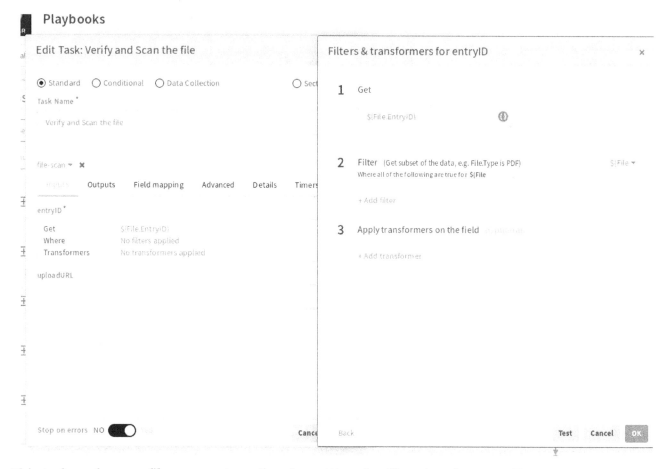

This task performs a file-scan automation, by getting the file using the entry ID

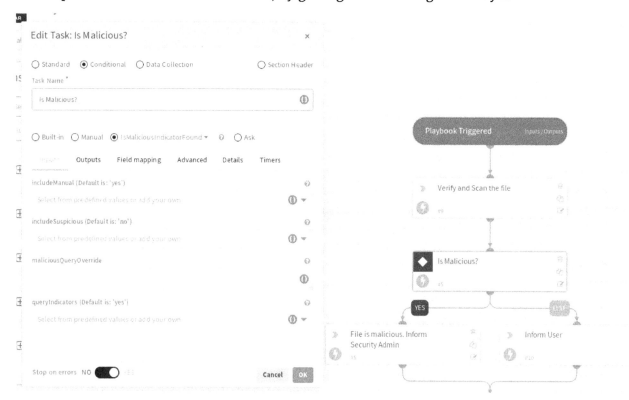

Next, I create a conditional task to check the decision based on the Maliciousness. It basically gives two branches with two options. Yes/no. Here I used the automation **IsMaliciousIndicatorFound.**

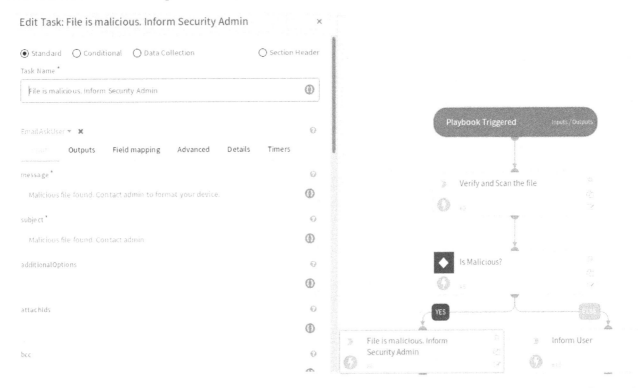

Then continues with two options. If the file is malicious, Inform the Security Admin. Or Else, Inform the User. We can customize the mail subject and body.

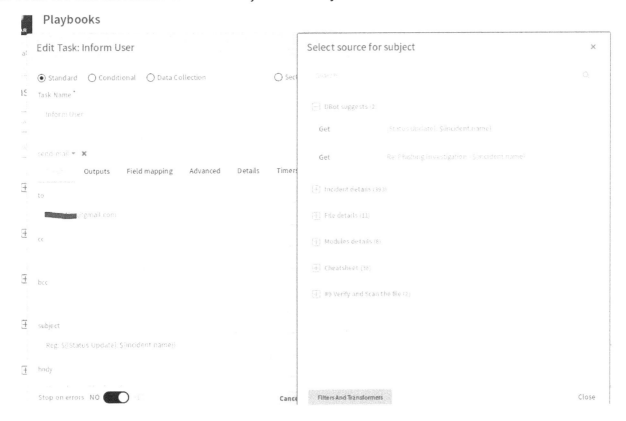

The else task is to inform the user. Mention the email id of the user directly. You can also put the command to get the email id directly as well. Customize the subject with incident status followed with the incident name. DBot is the Cortex XSOAR machine learning bot and it gives possible suggestions to the analyst.

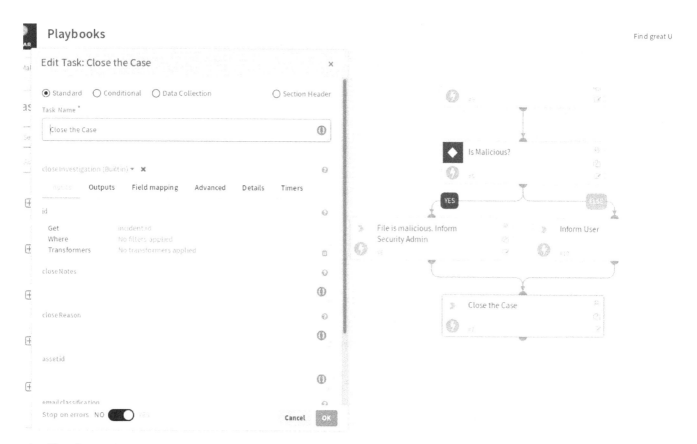

Finally Close the Case. I used the built-in **closeInvestigation** automation to fulfil the action. Now the playbook is created. Let's create the incident manually and perform the investigation using this playbook.

11.2 Incident Creation

A new incident can be created from the incidents page or from the dashboard.

Since this is created manually, we need to provide all the details. Name of the Incident **Malware file on SecOps Manager's Thumbdrive.** Type is Malware. Provide a date and time of event occurrence. Then select the playbook **Malware_Playbook_Updated.**

Edit: 'Malware file on SecOps Manager's Thumbdrive ' of type 'Malware_Jaa'   ×

⊟ Basic Information

Name:

Malware file on SecOps Manager's Thumbdrive

Occurred: Reminder: Owner:

February 15, 2021, 7:40 PM   Choose time and date   Admin ✖

Role: Type: Severity:

Administrator ✖ Analyst ✖   ▼   Malware_Jaa   🌑 Unknown

Playbook: Labels: Phase:

Malware Playbook Updated ▼   2   Unassigned

Details:

Malware file on SecOps Manager's Thumbdrive . File attached

Reset form   Cancel   Update Incident

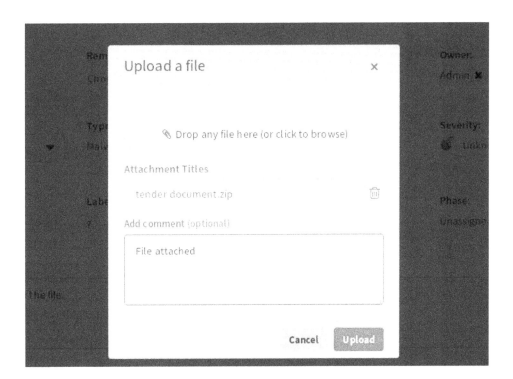

Attach the suspicious file. This is the incident attachment. Then create in incident.

11.3 Incident Investigation

Start the investigation of the incident. The first tab is the case Info. It shows the summary of the current incident. Note that the Playbook settings of the incident type was previously set to run automatically. Because of this, the incident investigation has already run in the background without any manual intervention.

Go to the investigation page to view the details.

The indicators in the incidents are auto extracted. Here the indicator is the attachment file. VirusTotal has provided the reputation of the file scan, and you can view that from the investigation page.

Since the file is a genuine malware (EICAR), the reputation is bad.

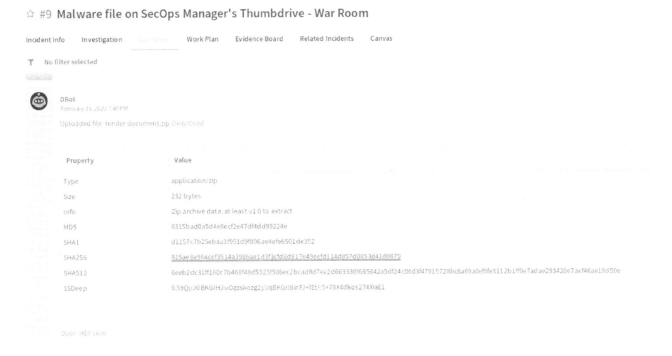

The War room shows all the task results of the playbook. In here, you can see a red double underline under the SHA256 value. Red double underline means that the reputation is bad.

The VirusTotal scan result also shows the reputation as Bad. We can click the value to see the indicator information. 4@9 is the entry ID of the file attachment. Just like an identifier.

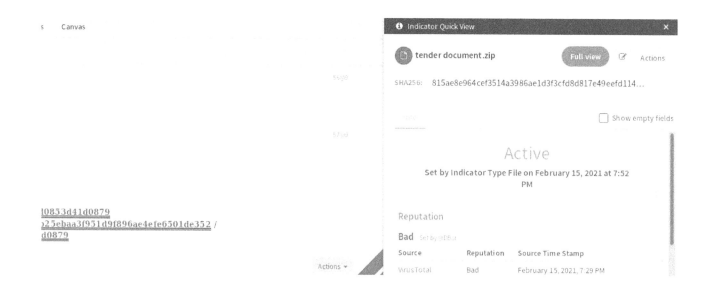

Now let's examine the playbook status.

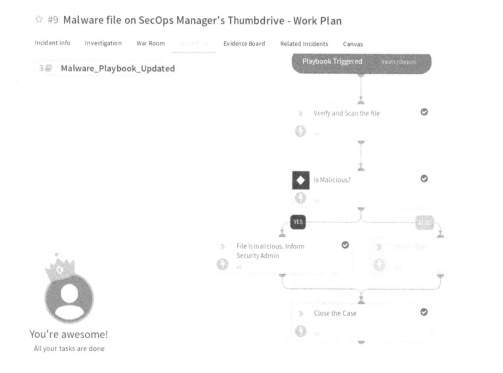

We can click on each task to view the status and results. Let's examine the tasks one by one.

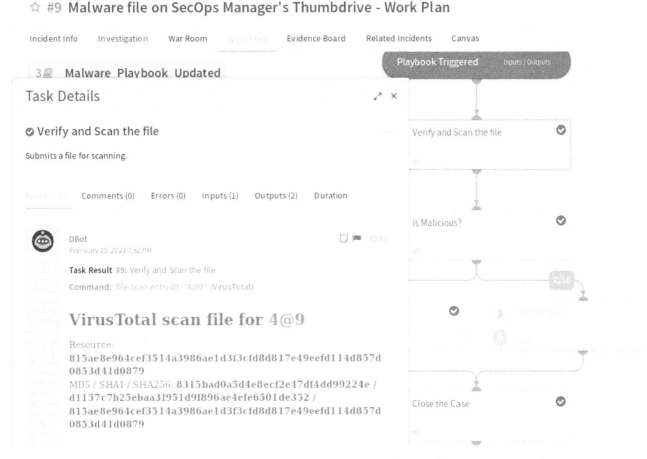

We can see the input, output and the results of the task. The results are updated in the war room as well. The task **Verify and Scan** the file gives the scan results of the file from VirusTotal integration. Note that, if VirusTotal instance is not installed, it will throw error.

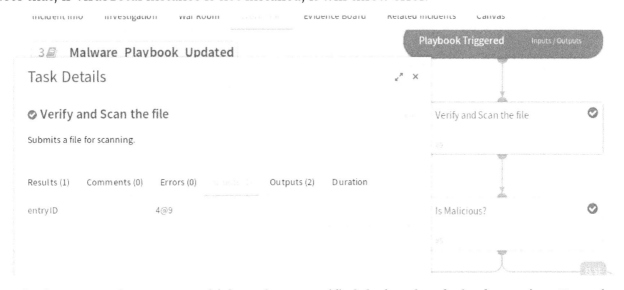

So, the input was the entryID, which we have specified during the playbook creating. Here, for this incident attachment, the entryID value is 4@9.

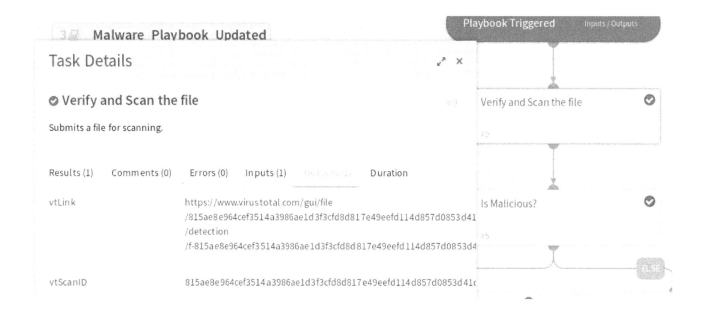

Output is the result returned from VirusTotal. The VirusTotal integration communicate with its server in the internet using API.

The next task is to validate whether the file is malicious or not. Here in this case, the file is malicious. Hence the Conditional Task returned the result **Yes.**

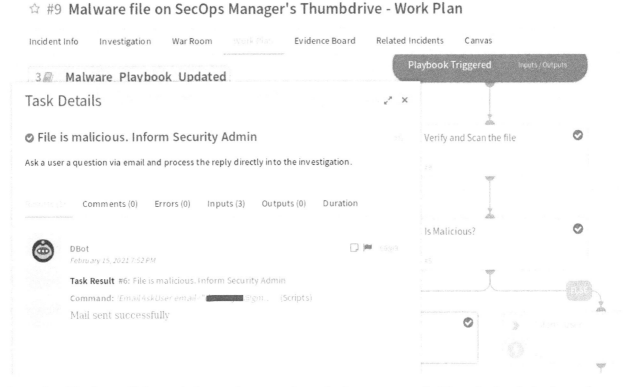

Since the file is malicious, inform the security admin over email. The playbook task performs this automatically and to fulfil this, your XSOAR must have the Mail-Sender Integration. Or else, the mail cannot be sent.

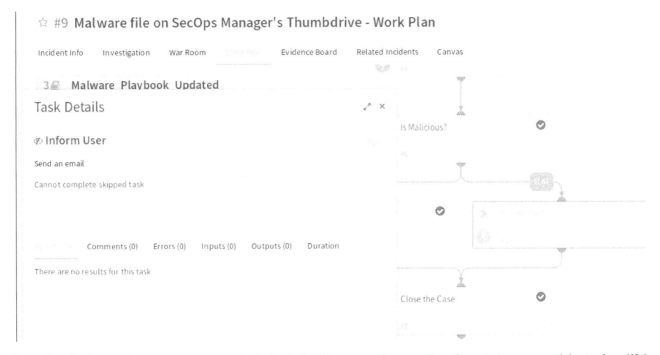

If we check the Inform user task, which is faded because it was the else statement. This task will be executed only if the file was clean. Hence it is mentioned as skipped.

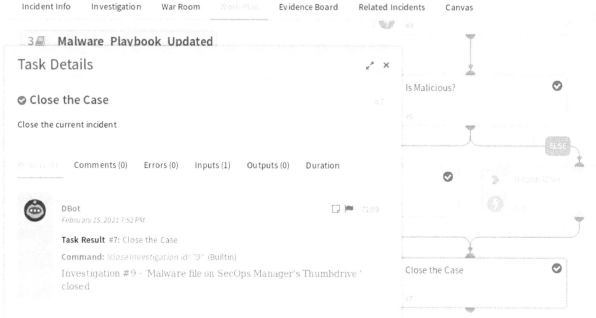

Finally, the case has been closed. Let's visit the War room once again.

We can see the playbook task results here as well. The mail status and subject, all such information we can see from the war room page. At the user end, they receive the email from Cortex XSOAR.

Malicious file found. Contact admin – #9 3686e4bb

Jaacostan Cortex XSOAR ▆▆▆▆acostan.com via ▆▆▆▆▆t.com

to me ▾

Malicious file found. Contact admin to format your device.

DBot
February 15, 2021 7:52 PM

Command: *!GenerateInvestigationSummaryReport name="Investigation Summary" type="pdf"* (Scripts)

Returned file: report_Investigation_Summary_1613436763017439144.pdf Download

DBot
February 15, 2021 7:52 PM

Close Notes

Close Reason

Duration   6m14s

The generation of the incident report was configured as a post-processing script. Hence an investigation summary report was generated by XSOAR automatically and is available to download from the war room.

This page intentionally left blank.

12. Demo: Block Malicious IP in Firewall.

The objective of this demo is to illustrate how Cortex XSOAR can be collaborated with other products in your environment to perform certain actions. In this demo, I integrate Cortex XSOAR with Palo Alto firewall. I create a manual incident to block a malicious IP and XSOAR orchestrates and automate the action to add a firewall rule to block the malicious IP.

Note that, the IP address I used here is a random one and just for the demonstration purpose and may not be malicious in real.

To make this demo work, first install the PAN-OS content pack. This is needed to create the Palo Alto firewall integration instance. Go to the Marketplace and install the required Content Pack.

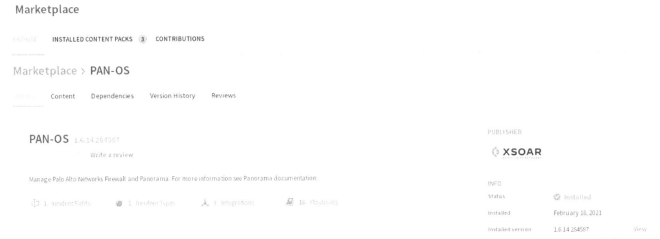

The PAN-OS content pack has been installed. You can explore more on the contents of the pack. There are one new incident field, one incident type, one integration and 16 playbooks come along with this installation.

Go to the integration page to create an instance. The integration name is Palo Alto Networks PAN-OS.
Click on Add instance.

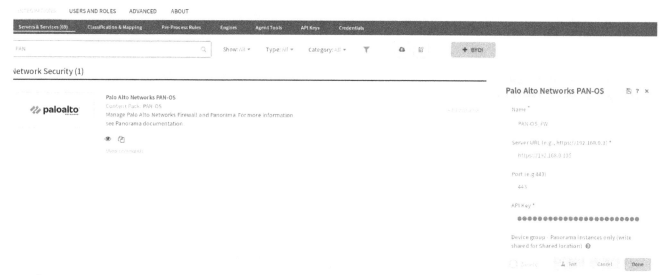

Configure the instance by providing the Firewall details. Mention the firewall IP, port and they communicate over API. So, provide the API key.

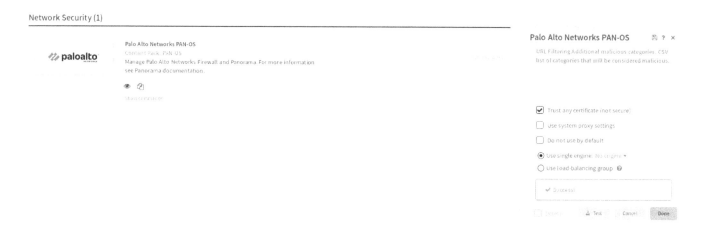

Validate your configuration and click on Done. The integration instance has been successfully created.

If you want to validate the integration manually, you may manually try to create a firewall rule using the integration command.

Most of the commands installed along with the PAN-OS integration begins with **panorama-**. Here to create a new rule, I used **panorama-create-rule** command.

```
!panorama-create-rule rulename="Test XSOAR" description="Test Rule from XSOAR"
action="deny" source="any" destination="1.1.1.1" source_zone="inside"
destination_zone="outside" service="any" disable="No" application="ssh"
source_user="any"
```

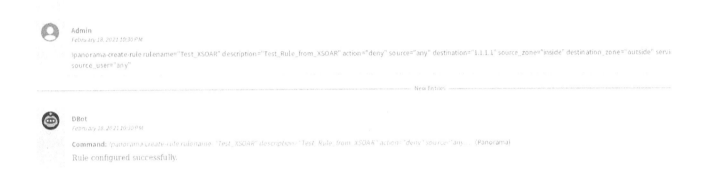

The result of the commands will be displayed as well. Here the Rule configured successfully. We can verify this from the Firewall GUI.

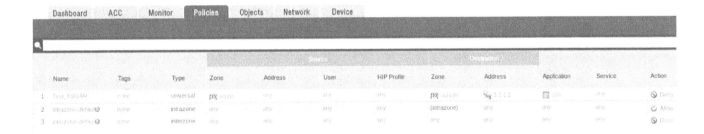

Now the same task, we want to automate. For this, we need to create a playbook for the automation and orchestration. Let's create a Playbook.

12.1 Playbook Creation

To create a playbook, go to the Playbooks page, and create new.

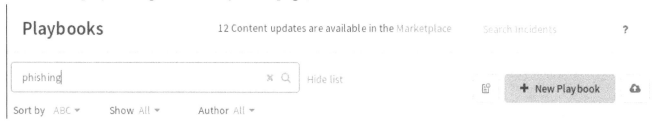

Give a name for the playbook.

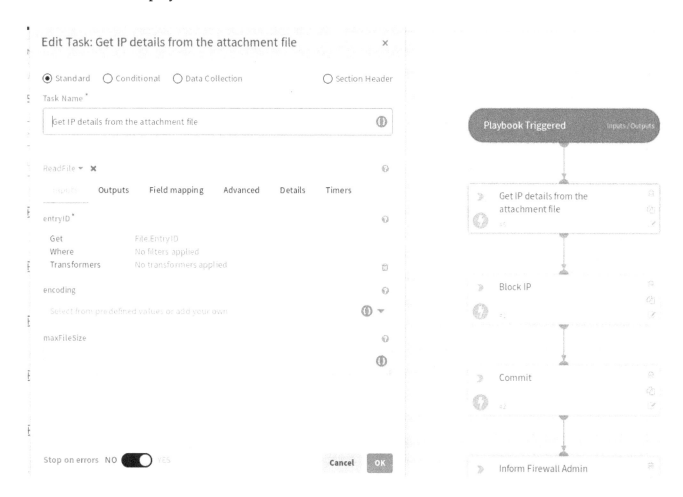

I will explain the tasks one by one. The first task is to get the IP details from the incident attachment file. For this, when I create the incident manually, I need to attach a text file with the IP address which I want to block.

The task "Get IP details from the attachment file" used the automation script "ReadFile" to read the incident attachment using the file EntryID.

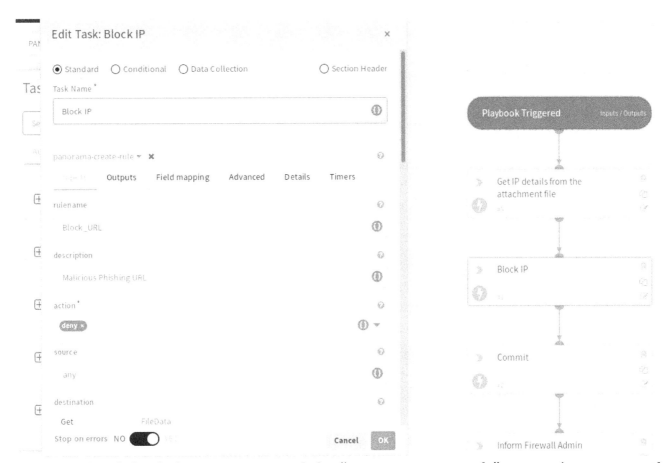

The second task is Block IP. Here we used the "panorama-create-rule" automation to create the block rule. Give a rule name "Block_URL" and an optional description. Specify the action as "deny". Source is "any" and the destination is the IP extracted from the incident attachment file.

Get the fileData and if you want to do some transformation or filtering, that can be mentioned in the rule. For example, you may use the regex to extract only IP address from the attachment file.
Here in this demo, I used transformers rule to remove all white spaces.

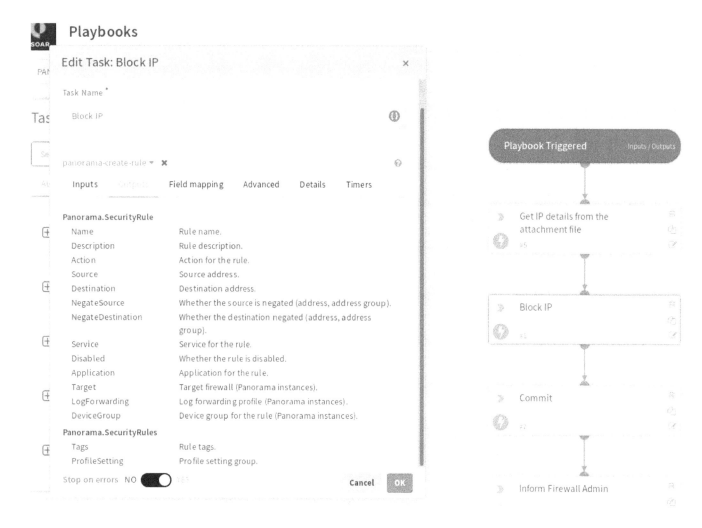

So, what is the output of this task.? In the Outputs tab, we can see all the details related to the task output. Since this is using an automation script, it creates a security rule with the gathered input.

The third task is to perform the Commit action in the firewall. Commit is a Palo Alto firewall team to apply the particular change. Here after the rule create, we need to commit to apply the block rule.

For this, use another standard task. And use the **panorama-commit** command. Not input is required for this particular task,

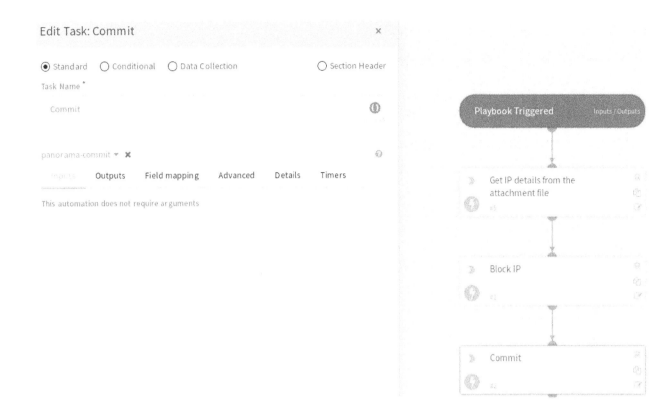

The next task is to send a mail to inform the firewall admin about the change.

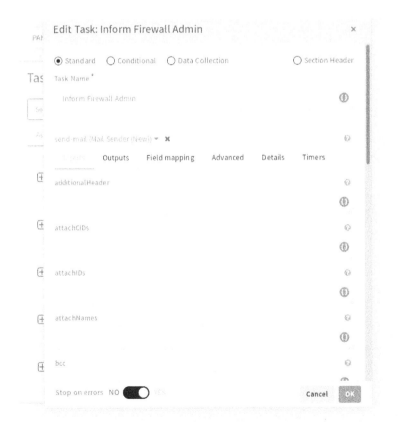

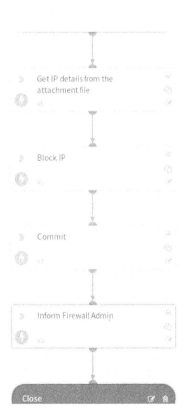

And the last task, just a section header Close.

Now the playbook has been successfully created. Let's create an incident

12.2 Incident Creation

I am creating the incident manually. Go to the incidents page and create a new incident.

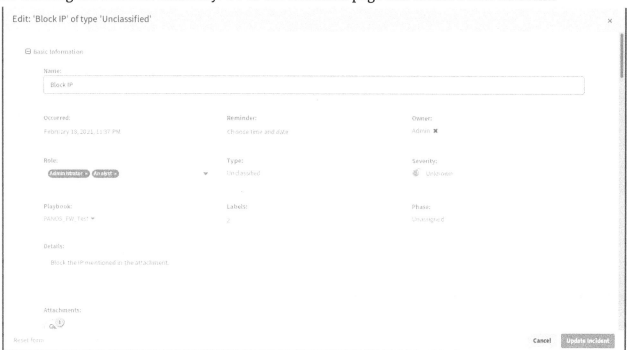

Give the required details. I gave the incident name as Block IP, mentioned the date and time, attached the Playbook "PANOS_FW_Test".

Add an attachment that contains the IP details. The dummy IP address which we want to block is 1.1.2.2.

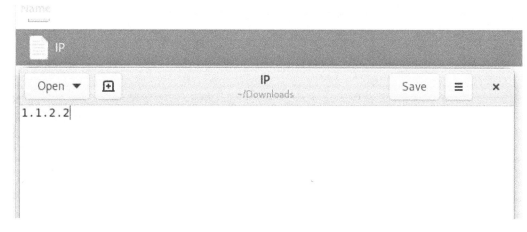

Also note that, based on the layout, you can mention the IP address details directly in the incident details. But for this demo, I just want to illustrate how the data can be read and used as a task input.

12.3 Incident Investigation

Start the Incident investigation process. The info page lists the summary of the incident.

You can see that the indicators are auto extracted. Here the only indicator is the attachment file.

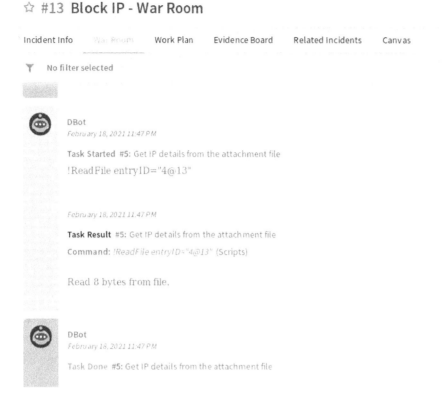

You can view the task details from the war room page. The incident attachment file has been read and IP address detail is extracted.

You can view the actual automation command with the details and the status of each task as well. The next task was the commit. From the War Room, you can see the commit action status, the Job ID etc.

DBot
February 18, 2021 11:47 PM

Task Started #2: Commit
!panorama-commit

February 18, 2021 11:47 PM

Task Result #2: Commit
Command: !panorama-commit (Panorama)

Commit:

JobID   14
Status Pending

DBot
February 18, 2021 11:47 PM

Task Done #2: Commit

And the final action is to send an email to the Firewall admin.

DBot
February 18, 2021 11:47 PM

Task Started #3: Inform Firewall Admin   Go to Task
!send-mail to="████████@gmail.com" subject="Closure for 13" body="Firewall Rule has been added for incident ID
13

Auto-generated." using-brand="Mail Sender (New)"

February 18, 2021 11:47 PM

Task Result #3: Inform Firewall Admin
Command: !send-mail to="████████@gmail.com" subject="Closure for 13" body="Firewall Rule has been added for incident I..." (Mail Sender (New))
Mail sent successfully

DBot
February 18, 2021 11:47 PM

Task Done #3: Inform Firewall Admin

The mail is sent to the Firewall admin using the Mail Sender integration. Note that, if the Mail Sender integration is not configured, XSOAR system cannot send any mails to the outside.
You can view the playbook status from the Work Plan page.

All the tasks have been completed successfully without any errors. Completed task are marked with a green tick icon. When the playbook is fully executed, XSOAR puts a You're awesome! Badge as well.

Now let's verify the results.

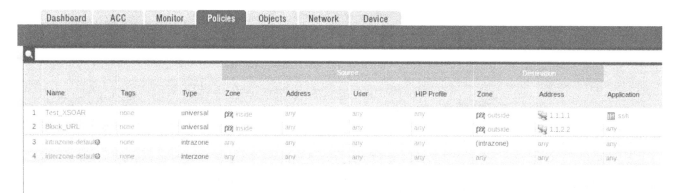

We can see that the Block_URL rule has been added in the firewall with the mentioned details. The destination IP address is 1.1.2.2, the same mentioned in the attachment file.

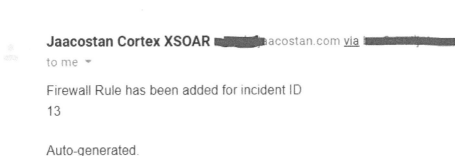

And finally, the firewall admin has received the automated mail and this was our final task.

Note that, all the three demonstration are extremely easy and basic. The only objective of these demonstrations is to illustrate the incident lifecycle process, how XSOAR does the Security Orchestration and Automation and how it helps in performing an incident investigation.

In the real world, you may create complex playbook but the fundamentals are the same. Task are the building blocks of a playbook. Each task performs a certain function. You combine multiple tasks together to achieve a larger broad result.

As a learner, you should practice creating different playbooks, adding various integrations to make yourself better in understanding the Cortex XSOAR orchestration and automation concepts clearly.

This page intentionally left blank.

13. Threat Intel Management (TIM)

Cortex XSOAR Threat Intel Management feature enables you to configure threat intel feed integration by ingesting and processing indicators. You can query indicators by reputation and analyze the reliability of their intelligence data source. Further you can integrate Threat Intel Management feature with other tools in your environment, such as Palo Alto Firewall EDL, where the XSOAR acts as the indicator feed provider to the other products in your organization.

Cortex XSOAR automates threat intel management by ingesting and processing indicator sources such as text/csv feeds and lists, and exporting the enriched intelligence data to the SIEMs, firewalls, and any other system that can benefit from the gathered indicator information. Cortex XSOAR can fetch indicators from either a vendor-specific source, such as AutoFocus, Talos or from a generic source using a CSV/Text feed or JSON file. You can export indicators as a hosted list, an EDL, or a TAXII collection. Exporting indicators enables your SIEM or firewall to ingest or pull the indicator list to update policy rules. The common indicator types include IP, URL, Domain, Email, File Hash, CVE, etc.

Cortex XSOAR can gather the indicator information from multiple sources and it is important to avoid duplication of information and keep track of the indicator expiry. When some indicators are no longer bad or its reputation changed, the same status should be updated in XSOAR as well. The indicator field Expiration Status displays the indicator status, Active or Expired. The indicator field Expiration displays the method by which and when that indicator is expired. Indicator expiration is applied at the indicator type level. Indicators assigned to a specific indicator type inherit the indicator type's expiration method.

One method is, you can define a job to trigger a playbook when the specified feed identifies a modification in the feed information. The modification can be a new indicator, a modified indicator, or a removed indicator.

Indicator Reputation.

An indicator's reputation is assigned according to the reputation returned by the source with the highest reliability. In cases where multiple sources with the same reliability score return a different reputation for the indicator, the worst reputation is taken. Indicators are assigned a reputation on a scale of 0 to 3. The table displays the indicator's reputation scores and the colors associated with each indicator's reputation.

Indicator Reputation		
Score	Colour	Reputation
0	No colour	None-No Reputation
1	Green	Good
2	Orange	Suspicious
3	Red	Bad

Source Reliability

The reliability of an indicator data source also determines the reputation of an indicator and the values for indicator fields when merging indicators. Indicator fields are merged according to the source reliability hierarchy. For example, when there are two different values for a single indicator field, the field will be populated with the value provided by the source with the highest reliability score. Reliability scores range from A to F.

Source Reliability	
A	Completely Reliable
B	Usually Reliable
C	Fairly Reliable
D	Not Usually Reliable
E	Unreliable
F	Reliability cannot be judged

13.1 Configuring a TIM feed Instance.

Cortex XSOAR can fetch indicators from either a vendor-specific source, such as AutoFocus, Talos or from a generic source using a CSV/Text feed or JSON file.

In this example, I am going to integrate a TIM text feed with Cortex XSOAR. There are a lot of free and paid threat intel feeds available in the internet. Here I am using a text feed from Openphish.com. Firstly, create the integration instance.

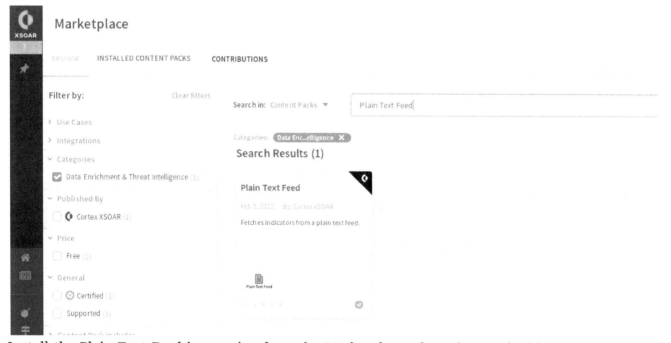

Install the Plain Text Feed integration from the Marketplace. If you have a feed in CSV format, you may install the CSV feed integration.

Now configure the integration instance.

Click on Add instance.

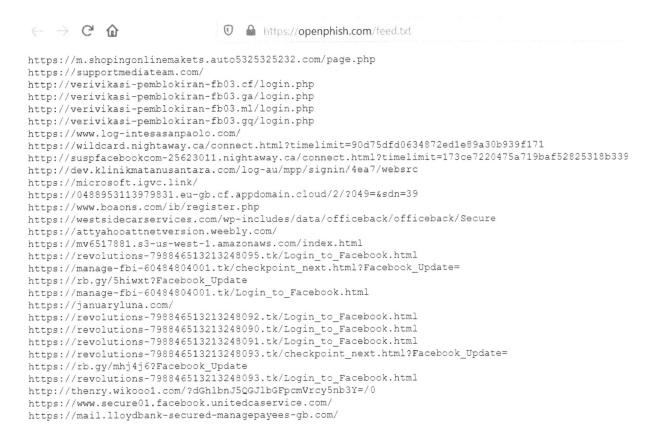

As I mentioned earlier, I am using the URL indicator feed from Openphish.com. The text feed is usually a large file and it keeps updated by the TIM provider.

In the instance settings, give a name for the instance "TIM_Text_Feed" and then select fetches indicator option to enable XSOAR to pull the data from the Indicator Source. Mention the feed URL. The text feed URL from Openphish is https://openphis.com/feed.txt

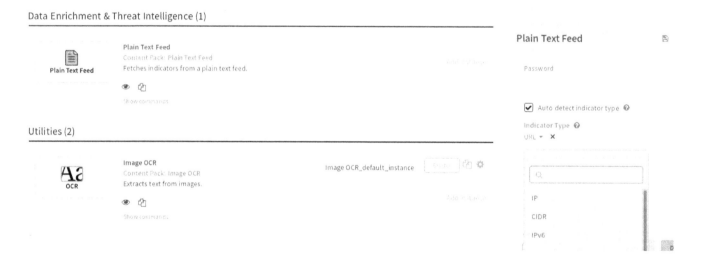

Select the Indicator type. Here the indicators are URL, hence selecting the type as URL.

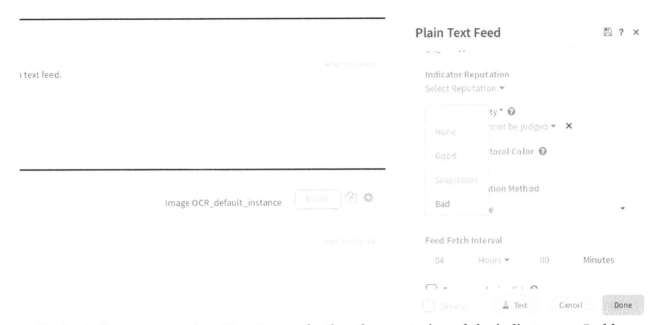

Specify the indicator reputation. Here I am selecting the reputation of the indicators as Bad because the feed I am using from Openphish is a list of bad URLs.

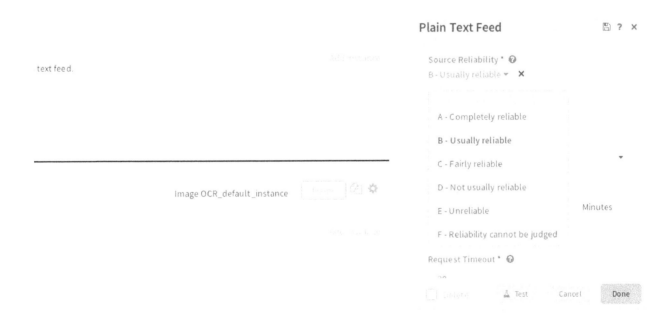

Specify the Source Reliability score. Here in this case, I select B–Usually Reliable.

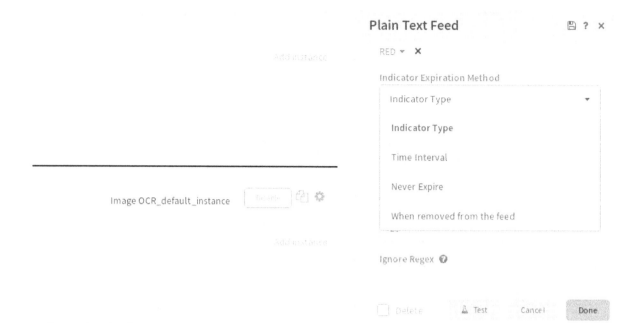

Now select the indicator expiration method. You can validate the indicatory expiry using time interval check, when removed from the feed or the indicators never expire.

Validate your settings and click on Done.

The instance has been successfully created and the feed has pulled 1585 indicators from the Source. These pulled indicators gets automatically added to the XSOAR indicator list and can be viewed from the Indicators page.

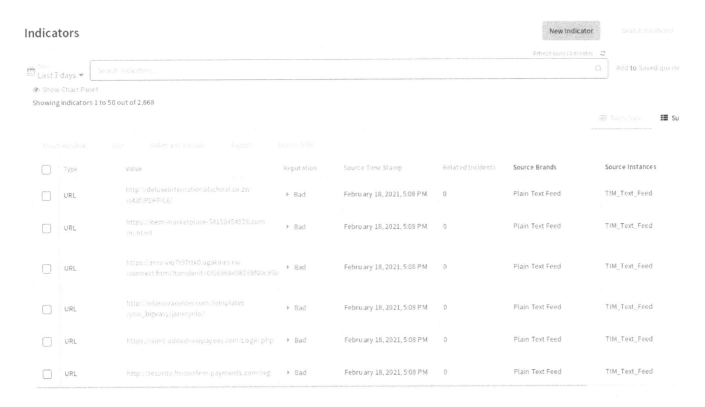

You can view the indicators, type the source of the indicators, reputation, expiration, incidents related to indicators etc. from this page. Click on the indicators to know more details about it.

If you want to add or edit indicator type, go to Settings > Advanced > Indicator Types.
To edit an existing indicator, select the indicator and click on edit.

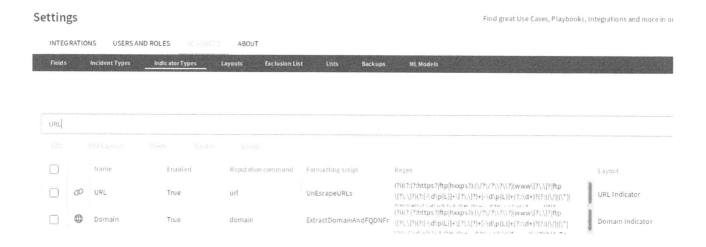

13.2 External Dynamic List (EDL) Integration

Cortex XSOAR has several Out-of-Box threat intelligence feed integrations and outbound feed integrations. Integrations such as AutoFocus, AWS, and Microsoft Azure enable collection of indicators. Example for an Outbound feed integrations is Palo Alto Networks PAN-OS External Dynamic List (EDL) Service and it enables XSOAR to provide the threat intel information to the Palo Alto firewalls, and can be used to create rules to control the traffic. You can also export indicators as a hosted list or a TAXII collection.

Let's see how to configure an EDL integration in Cortex XSOAR.

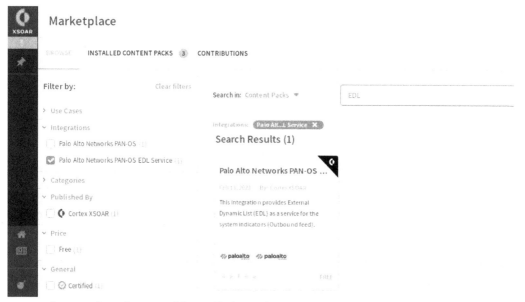

Go to the Marketplace and install the Palo Alto networks PAN-OS EDL Service content pack.
Then configure an Integration Instance to connect with the Palo Alto Firewall.

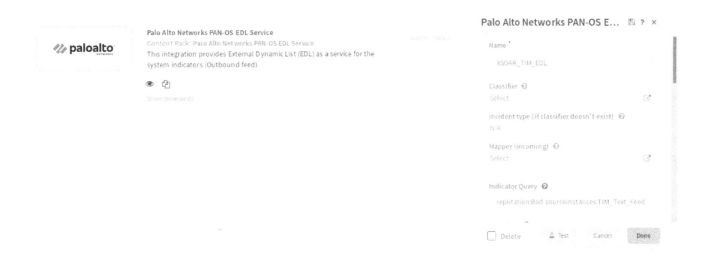

Give a name for the instance. Here you need to provide an Indicator Query. In XSOAR, there are a lot of indicators with different reputations. You don't need to export all those details to the external system. So, to filter the indicators, we use a search query. Let me illustrate how to get the Query string.

Go to the indicators page,

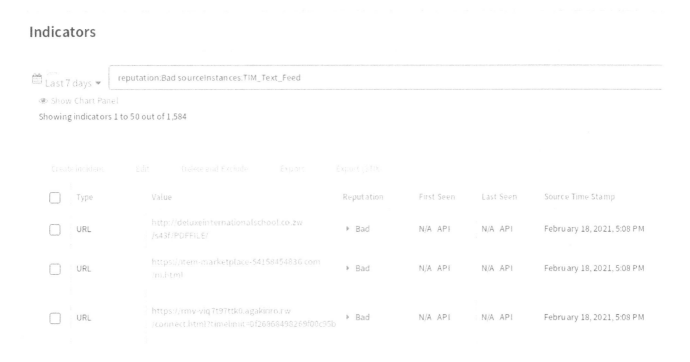

Here I want to filter the indicators based on the reputation and feed source. So, the query will be,
reputation:Bad sourceinstance:TIM_Text_Feed

Use this query string and paste it in the Indicatory Query Field.

Indicator Query ❓

reputation:Bad sourceInstances:TIM_Text_Feed

☐ Delete   🧪 Test   Cancel   **Done**

We are going to make this XSOAR server as an Indicator feed source. Means the other systems can grab listen to the feed and get the indicator list.

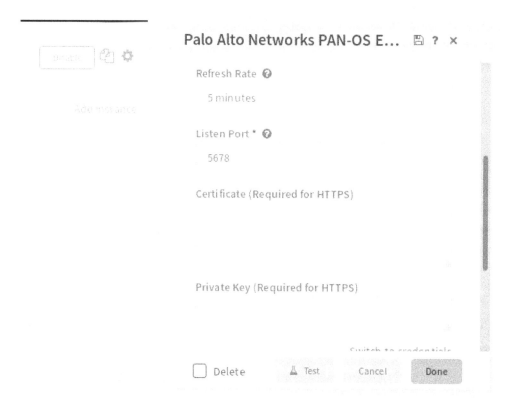

Palo Alto Networks PAN-OS E...   💾 ? ✕

Refresh Rate ❓

5 minutes

Listen Port * ❓

5678

Certificate (Required for HTTPS)

Private Key (Required for HTTPS)

Switch to credentials

☐ Delete   🧪 Test   Cancel   **Done**

I am settings the XSOAR server's listen port as 5678.
Validate your settings and click Done.

Data Enrichment & Threat Intelligence (1)

paloalto   Palo Alto Networks PAN-OS EDL Service
Content Pack: Palo Alto Networks PAN-OS EDL Service
This integration provides External Dynamic List (EDL) as a service for the system indicators (Outbound feed).   XSOAR_TIM_EDL   [Disable] ⚙

Add instance

The instance has been successfully created and the feed is now active.
To validate the feed manually, check the feed from your browser
http(s)://<Cortex _XSOAR_IP>:<port>

You can see the Indicator feed from the browser.
Now configure EDL in the Palo Alto Firewall.

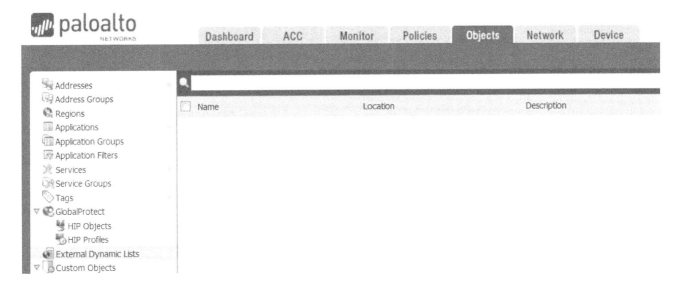

From the Palo Alto Firewall GUI, for to the External Dynamic Lists option. And create a new EDL.
Provide a name for the feed, type, and an optional description. Mention the EDL source URL.
Here in this case, the source URL is the IP of XSOAR server.
http://192.168.0.106:5678.

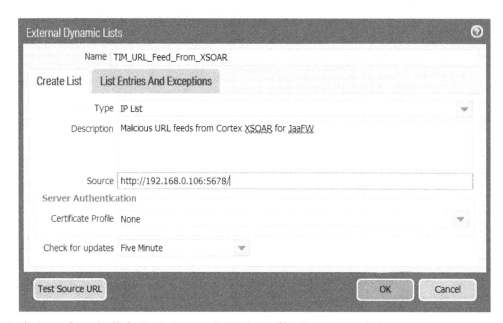

Set the update interval and click Test Source URL to validate your settings.

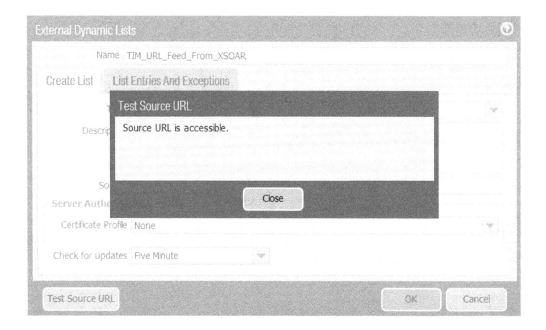

The source URL is accessible and Click OK to save the settings.

Name	Description	Source	Certificate Profile	Frequency
▽ **Dynamic IP Lists**				
TIM_URL_Feed_From_XSOAR	Malicious URL feeds from Cortex XSOAR for JaaFW	http://192.168.0.106:5678/	None	Five Minute

The EDL is now ready. The admin may use this list to create any rules in the firewall to block access to the malicious URLs mentioned in the EDL.

14. Reports

Reports contain information related to the incidents and the XSOAR server, which enables you to generate data in PDF, Word and CSV formats. A report template contains widgets to analyze the data in different formats such as graphs, pie charts, or text. Cortex XSOAR comes with out of the box reports, such as critical and High incidents, Daily incidents, last 7 days incidents, and so on. You cannot edit these inbuilt report templates except the schedule time and who can receive the report. However, if you want to change these types of reports, go to GitHub reports repository, download and update the JSON file and upload the report.

You can create and customize reports from the Reports page. Let's explore the report page and how to create a new report.

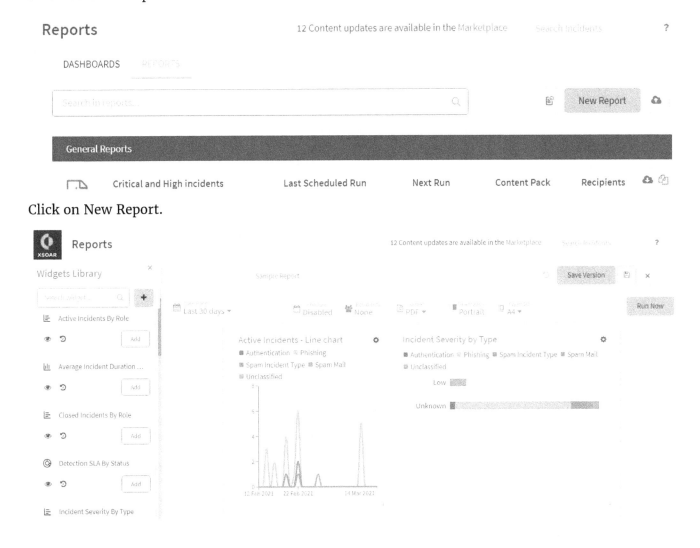

Click on New Report.

Give a name for the report. You can see all the available widgets in the widgets library. Select the required widget and add to your report page.

For this demo purpose, I have added two incident widgets, Active Incident-Line chart and Incident Severity by type.

You can customize the widget data by clicking the gear icon of the widget.

Further possible to edit the data query and the time frame. Click on Save to apply the changes.

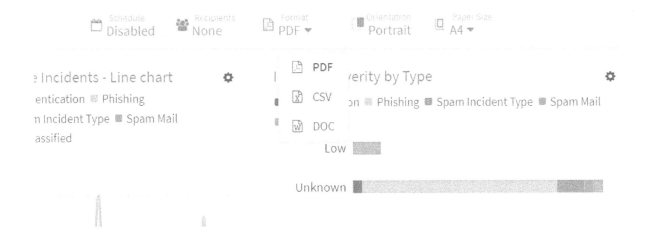

You can create the report in PDF, CSV and DOC format. Once all changes are made and the report is customized, click on Save version, give a comment and save.

You can also see a lot of out of the box system report templates in XSOAR. These reports are not customizable; however, you can change the date range and the details of the receiver.

You can click on the Run Now button to generate a report. A sample report is shown below.

15. Configure Backup

Cortex XSOAR offers two backup methods. Automated Backup and Live Backup. Let's talk about the Automated backup first.

15.1 Automated Backup

Cortex XSOAR backs up the database on a daily basis, by storing the entire database of incidents, playbooks, scripts, and user defined configurations. Automated backup is mainly used for on-demand system rollback and restore. Though the name of the backup is Automated, the actual process includes a little bit of manual tasks.

From the Settings > Advanced > Backups page, you can configure whether you want Cortex XSOAR to create automatic backups, and the location to store the backups. The database backup files are located in /var/lib/demisto/backup Every day Cortex XSOAR adds to its store of daily, weekly, and monthly backups files. Note that Artifacts and Attachments are not backed up. And therefore, it should be manually copied from the /var/lib/demisto.

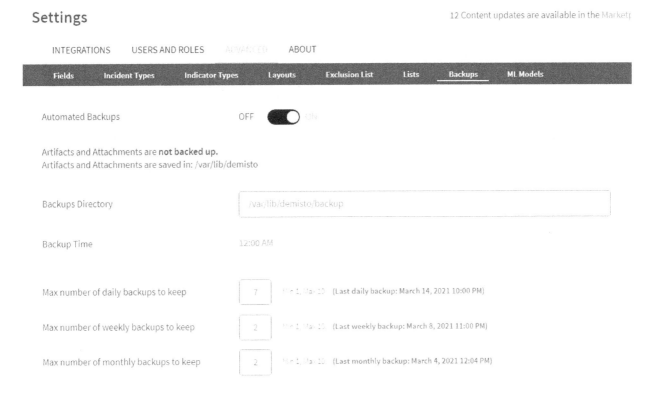

Steps to back up the database.

- Select Settings > Advanced > Backups > Automated Backups
- In the Backups Directory, mention the location for the backups directory.
- Set the time for the backup.
- Also define the maximum number of daily, weekly, and monthly backups to keep. It is recommended that you make a backup copy of the backup directory on a different machine.

And if you want to restore or rollback the database, perform the following steps in order.

- Log out all users from Cortex XSOAR.
- Stop the service.
- Delete the content of the database directory (default directory is /var/lib/demisto/data).
- Copy the backup file to the database location.
- Extract the .gzip backup file using tar –xzf <file-name>
- Move the demisto_XXXXX.db files to the partitionsData folder. Keep the demisto.db file in the /data parent folder.
- Restart the server and log in to Cortex XSOAR.

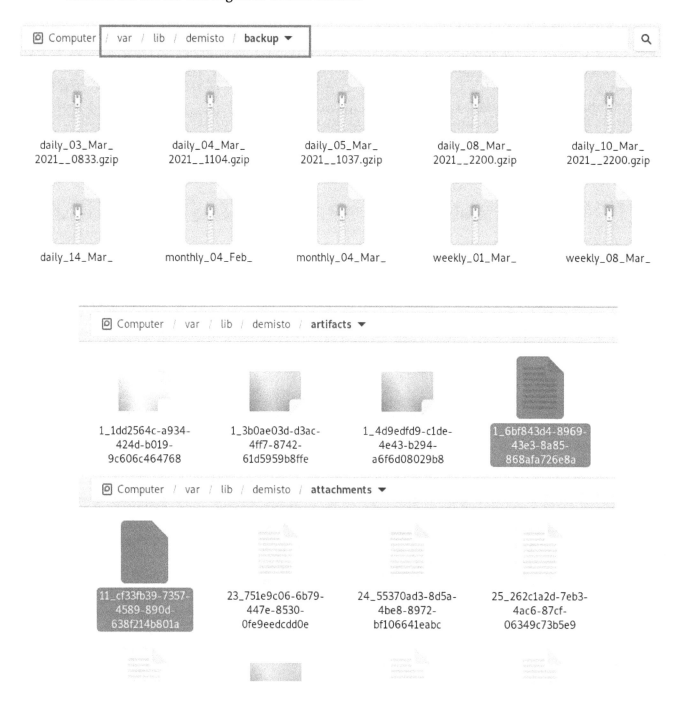

In addition of the database, the following directories need to be backed up and restored manually.

- /var/lib/demisto/artifacts
- /var/lib/demisto/attachments
- /var/lib/demisto/d2_server.key
- /var/lib/demisto/tools
- /var/lib/demisto/versionControlRepo
- /usr/local/demisto
- /etc/demisto.conf

15.2 Live Backup

Live Backup is the real time backup method in Cortex XSOAR and it enables you to mirror your production server to a backup server. In a disaster recovery situation, you can easily convert your backup server to be the production server. Server actions are mirrored in real time. However, there are certain limitations:

- Live Backup uses a single main server and a single standby server. Additional servers are not currently supported.
- Active/Active configuration is not currently supported.
- Each host retains its own distinct IP address and host name.
- Failover is not dynamic. In the event of a disaster, the administrator must make the secondary XSOAR server as Active
- In the event of a server failover, engines automatically reconnect to the active host.

By default, the Live Backup option is hidden. To enable it, Go to Settings > About > Troubleshooting Add a server configuration,

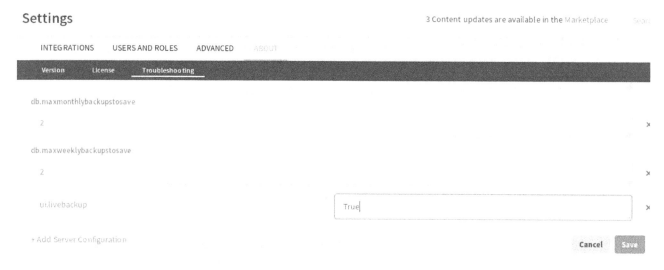

Add a custom parameter **ui.livebackup** and set the value **True.** Click Save

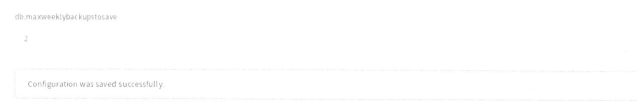

Now go to the Backups page, to configure the live backup configurations.

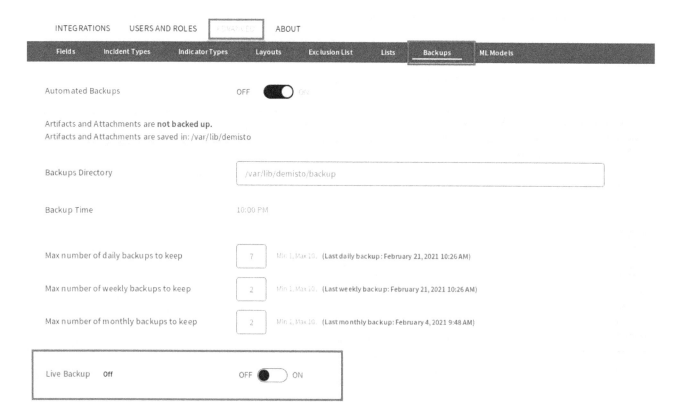

Now the Live Backup option shows up. Note that, this won't show up until you add the server configuration parameter from the troubleshooting page.

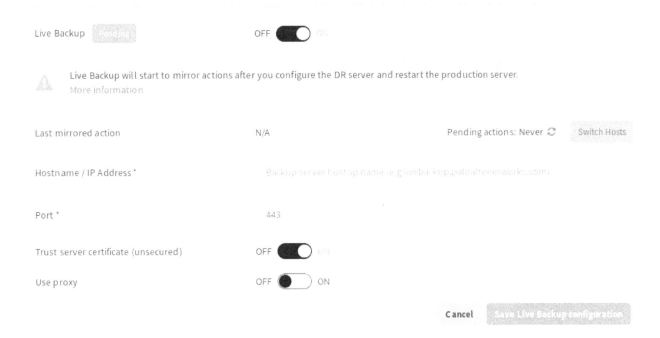

Toggle the button to ON and give the standby server's IP address and port details.
Click on Save Live Backup configuration to finish the configuration in the Active XSOAR server.

Now Set up the standby server.
It is recommended to setup the standby server in a different location, to achieve high availability in the case of a disaster. The standby server should be configured with a different host name or IP address.

- From the terminal install Cortex XSOAR using the -- -dr -do-not-start-server flag
  # ./demistoserver-xxxx.sh -- -dr -do-not-start-server
- Verify that the backup server is accessible from the production server through port 443 (default port) or any other port configured as a listening port.
- Stop the Cortex XSOAR server **sudo service demisto stop**
- Create a tarball file of the all the required files and folders on the production server to be copied to the backup server. Make sure that all files and folders have **demisto:demisto** ownership.
  #tar --ignore-failed-read -pczf demistoBackup.tgz /var/lib/demisto/data
  /var/lib/demisto/artifacts /var/lib/demisto/attachments /var/lib/demisto/systemTools
  /var/lib/demisto/d2_server.key /usr/local/demisto/cert* /usr/local/demisto/demisto.lic
- Copy the files and folders from the production server to the backup server. These files and folders are from the **/var/lib/demisto**

- Copy the created tarball file to the backup server. You may use scp or any other manual copy method.
- On the backup server, extract the backup tarball file.
  # tar -C / -xzpvf demistoBackup.tgz
- Start the backup server and then the production server.
  #sudo service demisto start
- If the communication and the procedure is successful, Live Backup is ON and you can view the status from the Backups page.

16. Introduction to Cortex XSOAR for MSSP

In a Managed Security Service Provider (MSSP) environment, multiple customers may have different kind of security tools from various vendors. Also, each tenant might have unique process, workflows and the compliance requirements might vary as well. Therefore, a SOAR solution for an MSSP should be flexible and scalable to accommodate the requirements of multiple tenants.

Cortex XSOAR multi-tenant deployments are designed for MSSPs that require strict data segregation between tenant accounts and the flexibility to easily share critical security data to the tenant accounts. Separate databases are maintained for each tenant, which helps to prevent data leakage. Cortex XSOAR for MSSPs facilitates the management of different tenants from a single console. Scalability features enables to deploy multiple servers on-premises or hosted cloud and across multiple geo locations. However, Multi-tenancy architecture is more complicated than Cortex XSOAR Enterprise server architecture. It requires more computing resources, DR requirements. The server maintenance is more complicated and requires a strong IT team. Therefore, Backup and restore, upgrade, Disaster Recovery are more complex than single-server deployments. In XSOAR, tenants are known as Accounts.

Cortex XSOAR for a MSSP environment, offers the following Service models.

1) Co-Managed: In this model, the customer has access to the infrastructure and the content. Both the MSSP and the customer have the access to the XSOAR solution and can manage the service.

2) Fully Managed: In this model, only the MSSP has the access to the Cortex XSOAR.

With the above Service models, there are two different deployment models as well.

1) One to One: In this model, One SOC is fully dedicated to one customer. This can be hosted wither at MSSP location or at the Customer Premises.

2) One to Many: In this model, One SOC serves multiple customers. And this is always hosted at MSSP's location.

In Cortex XSOAR, multi-tenancy is achieved by using three components. A master instance, Hosts and Engines.

Master.
Master Server is used for the administration of the SOAR environment. Access to all the tenants is done through the master instance. Means, Master instance is the front end for your XSOAR environment. You can also host the tenants in the master server directly as well, but it not recommended.

Hosts.
Hosts are physical Cortex XSOAR instances and this is where you configure the tenants. They act as a proxy to serve the tenant information with the Master Server Instance.

Engines.
Engines are instances running in your XSOAR environment where tenants cannot access integrations. Engines are used to extend the server capabilities and can load-balance integrations.

The Cortex XSOAR deployment lifecycle for MSSP.

1) Plan the deployment. Take a decision on the deployment plan based on the Service model, tenant size and location. The hardware requirements should be also taken in to the consideration. Each tenant must meet the hardware requirements of CPU, memory, and storage.

The hardware requirements for the master server are based on the number of tenants. For each tenant, minimum 16 core CPU and 32 GB RAM is required. For example, if there are 4 tenants, then the Master server requirement will be 4*16 core CPU, 4*32 GB RAM.

For Host server, minimum 8 core CPU (16 recommended) and 16 GB RAM (32 recommended).

2) Install and license Cortex XSOAR and setup network connectivity to the Cortex XSOAR server.

3) Add Hosts as per scaling requirements and add tenants easily under account management. Note that, the Accounts management option is visible only when you installed your Cortex XSOAR server with the -- -**multi-tenant** flag.

4) Since the MSSP environment contains multiple tenants and a lot of analysts. Some might be dedicated to one tenant. So, Setup roles for analysts based on their responsibilities. Also, setup customized roles for tenant users in co-managed model.

5) Customize the Dashboard. Dashboards can be customized at tenant level whereas Integrations, playbooks and rules can be configured at a master or tenant level.

17. Cortex XSOAR job roles.

Palo Alto Cortex XSOAR environment defines three different job roles.

1) IT Administrator

   The job responsibilities of an IT administrator include, the installation of the XSOAR platform components (Server, hosts, engines), monitors, maintains, and troubleshoots the system

2) Security Analyst

   Security Analysts are the ones who perform the Incident investigation. They can create, Assign and manage the cases and they perform everything from the GUI. The access privilege for each analyst is based on Role Based Access Control. The security analysts use the War Room to perform investigations and to collaborate with other analysts.

3) SOAR Engineer

   SOAR engineer enables and configures integrations, creates custom incident types and layouts, Creates and deploy automations and playbooks.

However, if you want to be good in Cortex XSOAR solution, you must build up your skills and knowledge level and ensure you can meet the following requirements. These skills are extensively tested in the Palo Alto Networks Certified Security Automation Engineer (PCSAE) exam.

- Make sure you can differentiate automation commands, scripts, system commands, search queries.
- Make sure you know the syntax and format of the commands.
- Have a basic idea on troubleshooting integrations, playbooks etc.
- Practice creating dashboards and reports.
- Explore market place and integrations.
- Learn to create integrations, instances and explore each option.
- Learn how to create a playbook, tasks and use additional functions such as filters/transformations.
- Learn to read war room entries properly.
- Have a thorough understanding on XSOAR architecture, Live Backup, Distributed Database, MSSP, dev-prod, Engines. How it communicates and what are its functions etc.
- Understand how to create users and roles, set RBAC permissions.
- Thorough understanding about incident types, Indicator types and its creations.
- Thorough understanding on Threat Intel Management.

18. Summary

The security professionals in a SOC faces various problems such as alert fatigue, false alerts flooding, gaps in collaboration and importantly human errors. Automating the incident investigation and response can reduce the human errors to a minimum. Therefore, a platform like SOAR is very important for a SOC. The SOAR offering from Palo Alto is known as Cortex XSOAR and it ingests events/alerts from external sources such as SIEMs, log servers, monitoring tools, other security tools like Firewalls, IPS etc.) and respond to these alerts by executing an automated process-driven playbook and thereby performing the Incident Investigation in an automated, quick and organized manner. A SOAR platform integrates your organization's security and monitoring tools, helping you centralize, standardize your incident handing processes. It automatically correlates security alerts from external sources against threat intelligence feeds for bad indicators, integrates malware analysis into incidents after detonating in a sandbox or submitting to a third party for analysis.

In this book, we have gone through the solution architecture, detailed step by step installation of the XSOAR application, and the configuration of Cortex XSOAR. We have seen how the integrations and playbook automations help the analysts to close the incidents in a standardized and quick manner. The War Room provides an arena for collaboration, helps the analysts to collaborate with other analysts to get more information and inputs.

The incident lifecycle in Cortex XSOAR includes a lot of tasks such as creation of fields, layouts, incident types, and with the use of playbooks, the incidents are thoroughly investigated, and closed. Report generation is another feature of Cortex XSOAR. Reports can be generated when an incident is closed or manually based on the desired data and time period.

We have also seen how to develop a playbook and how it can be used for incident investigation. The incident investigation in Cortex XSOAR was illustrated with demos, which provides the learner an overall idea about the XSOAR capabilities such as orchestration, automation and response.

Cortex XSOAR Threat Intel Management feature enables you to configure threat intel feed integration by ingesting and processing indicators. In the final sections, we have discussed how to perform the backup of Cortex XSOAR. I have covered almost all-important topics related to Cortex XSOAR in this book. And I hope the step-by-step illustrations of each Cortex XSOAR features and process, were easy to follow.

I hope this book was informative to you and I wish all the best to you. Thank you.

Appendix: Useful Links

I have consolidated some of the important links related to Cortex XSOAR and learnings, together in my website. You can scan the QR code and access the details. Happy Learning.

Check my other works on Amazon.

Author page amazon.com/author/jithinalex

Book	Description
	Network Automation using Python 3: An Administrator's Handbook Buy from Amazon: **https://www.amazon.com/dp/B084GFJB41/**
	Cisco Firepower Threat Defense (FTD) NGFW: An Administrator's Handbook: A 100% practical guide on configuring and managing Cisco FTD using Cisco FMC and FDM. Buy from Amazon: **https://www.amazon.com/dp/1726830187**
	Incident Handling and Response: A Holistic Approach for an efficient Security Incident Management. Buy from Amazon: https://www.amazon.com//dp/B089CWQVSV/

www.ingramcontent.com/pod-product-compliance
Lightning Source LLC
LaVergne TN
LVHW081755050326
832903LV00027B/1951